Then I Was Taken

A Memoir

203,000 people are taken each year.
What if you were one of them?

Then I Was Taken

A Memoir

Alaina Davis

203,000 people are taken each year.
What if you were one of them?

Then I Was Taken

Rose Gold Publishing, LLC

For my daughter, I promise that I will always protect you from the monsters, whether under the bed, or out in the world.

Dear Reader,

Before we begin, I want to warn you; this story's contents may be hard for some to read. My life has been filled with truly awful events, which I will share in time. I tried to kill myself at one point to make it all stop. Some days, even now, I ache to feel the simple hunger or cold that came from being homeless. For now, you need to know that in the following years, those first hardships I experienced would seem like a walk in the park.

What I am about to share with you are my raw, unfiltered memories of being kidnapped. Some parts have been filled in with details as closely as I can remember to being the truth, and therefore may not be completely accurate, but everything is the truth from my memory and perspective.

As I write, I won't disclose my location, or any real names, for I still fear for my safety. But I need to share my story, my whole truth, with you because I have learned something fundamental - monsters don't always live under the bed, and sometimes they are much closer than one may think.

I hope that you can read with an open mind and find something positive in all the darkness.

Sincerely,

Alaina

PROLOGUE

I'm cold.

And hungry.

I sit in the worn-down passenger seat of mom's van; the soft leather caresses my small frame, providing little protection from the freezing air. We are parked in front of a rundown McDonald's, in Independence, Oregon, waiting for my dad to pick me up. The lack of warmth from the van's sputtering heater makes time pass slowly.

My lunch of a hard-boiled egg does nothing to sate my hunger, but mom told me earlier that she can't buy more food. I'm not going to bother her by asking again. I chew and watch out the frosted window. Waiting.

The radio is playing, but the song is too filled with static to make out. The hum of mom's voice melts together with my loud shivering.

I wish dad would hurry.

His car is nice and warm, and I don't have to sleep in it unless I want to. I swallow the last bite of rubbery egg white, and my stomach grumbles in protest. I take a deep breath in to quiet it.

When I exhale, a white cloud forms in front of my face. I giggle a bit, "Look at this, Mom!" I take another breath in and expel it quickly. Waving my fingers through the steam in front of my face prompts a peal of laughter that makes mom smile. After experimenting with the cold air for a couple more minutes, I scoot further back into my seat to wait some more.

I wish we could play in the park.

My eyes start to feel heavy as I imagine flying through the air on a swing.

Before sleep takes me, mom shakes my shoulder and points out the window. "Look, Alaina! There he is!" I peek out and see that dad is driving his new white sedan, and his new wife, Linda, is with him. I bounce out of the van before mom can stop me and run to meet the shiny car as it parks up.

Dad grins at me when I jump up for a hug. The top of my head barely meets his hip, so I must wait for him to lift me up for a proper embrace. I wrap my small arms around his large frame and enjoy the feeling of his weekend stubble on my forehead when he kisses me. Anne steps up behind me and nods at dad, "Simar," she says curtly. Dad nods back and asks, "How's it going, Anne?" Instead of answering, she turns on her heel to climb back into the van.

Dad buckles me into his car before following to speak to her. I can't make out what they are saying, but he looks annoyed. I'm too excited to see him and Linda to care.

*****

As we drive home, after picking up dinner, I get asked the standard post-visit questions.

"Did you have fun?"

"Did you eat today?"

"Did you sleep in the car again?"

I answer everything as well as I can, between bites of warm food. After they seem satisfied, I start asking Linda and dad questions about since I've been gone. Of course, I'm mostly worried about how my toys are.

When we pull into our new driveway, dad gets out and walks inside, leaving my stepmom and I in the car. "Linda, can you help unbuckle, please?" She turns around to unclip the car seat buckle on my chest and pauses, "You know, you can call me *Mom* if you'd like."

I stop and think for a moment. "What about mom?"

"You can call her whatever you want, or you can call me whatever you want; it's just a suggestion."

We walk inside while I contemplate. This is a lot to take in. I never knew mom and dad could be called anything else. After a long while, I think of what to call my mom – *The other mom.*

*****

The title 'other mom' ended up sticking. As I spent more time at dad's house through my third and fourth birthday, I saw less of the other mom, Anne. Sleeping in the car for five nights a week turned into just three nights, then one, then none. I didn't understand at the time, but dad was winning sole custody of me. The other mom would only have limited visitation rights by the time I turned five.

Visits became few and far between. 'Linda' became 'Mom.' I gained sisters and a brother through her marrying my dad, and they would take time to play with me and make sure I was happy. Life seemed good through it all.

Nineteen years later, I recognize that things were not so good. I was homeless before dad earned custody. The other mom was too poor to care for me, and she had an extensive criminal record that prevented her from having a house.

Part One

1

AN INTRODUCTION

Before we start, I need to introduce you to my biological mother, Anne. A short-statured, overweight woman, she has bright red hair, green eyes, and three moles on the right side of her face, which are oddly in the same placement as Orion's belt. On the surface, Anne seems like a good person. She's outspoken, she'll listen to your problems, offer moral support, and even volunteer to help you move on a Saturday. It appears that she does everything she can to take care of her kids. If you look at her social media pages, she is a successful business coach that travels the world, dabbles in the divine, and offers free tarot readings. But just under that kind and caring façade is Anne, the criminal.

She had a wild streak and enjoyed breaking rules from a young age. At ten, she took her sister, who was three years younger, to throw flaming paper bags of feces at houses in the neighborhood. When caught, she pushed the blame away from herself and evaded punishment.

At age thirteen, she snuck out of the house nightly to try out different black magic spells and 'hex' her parents. Her dad passed away soon after Anne took up her new hobby, which spurred her to continue practicing.

At fifteen years old, Anne finally dropped out of school without her widowed mother's knowledge and spent her school hours in the baseball dugout, experimenting with various drugs. The bad habits got worse as time went on.

When Anne was 17, she was caught stealing from a local convenience store and was charged with theft. At the court hearing, a kind county judge felt sorry for the young girl standing trial alone - for what he felt was a silly teenage mistake. He didn't want her to suffer from a criminal record for stealing something worth the cost of a lunch at a local burger joint. Anne was sentenced to community service, in the form of painting a mural, and therapy.

The lax sentencing proved to be a mistake. Anne was diagnosed with Bipolar Disorder by the psychiatrist. She skipped out on the rest of her required therapy and never completed her volunteer service, going on her way with no record of the theft.

Less than a year later, Anne married her high school sweetheart, Scott. The couple found work for a small local business and had two sons a few years apart. Life seemed to be going great for Anne as a young woman and looking in from the outside; it seemed she had the perfect little family.

Unfortunately, that wasn't the case. Anne and Scott had a rocky relationship from the start. A year into their marriage, he would attempt to file for divorce - Until Anne showed him a positive pregnancy test. The two stayed together for the sake of their first son. As soon as their relationship started going downhill again, the couple found out Anne was pregnant for a second time.

Little did he know, Anne had an awful fear of being alone. Partly due to her diagnosis, and partly due to the fact she had no family or friends nearby, she felt that she needed her husband to rely on. While her husband thought the pregnancies were flukes, she had gone behind his back and stopped taking her birth control. She flushed the pills so he wouldn't know that she was doing everything she could to force him to stay.

Eventually, Scott became aware of the manipulation. When their oldest boy was five, Anne's husband left her. She lost her job, her house, and custody of her kids. With nowhere to go and no resources, Anne turned back to theft. Stealing clothing and food enabled her to live on her own for a short time until she met my dad, Simar.

My dad was a brilliant engineer from India, who immigrated to the United States to start his own company. He was looking for an assistant in San Jose, California, and Anne seemed to fill the role perfectly. Dad hired her immediately after meeting, not knowing anything about her past. They worked together for a short time before their relationship became less than professional.

Anne moved into dad's apartment soon after she was hired. In the first year that the two lived together, she managed to steal over $15,000 from him through his payroll system.

In the second year of their relationship, she compiled twice that in debt on his credit cards. Dad didn't know that Anne was stealing from him but started talking about leaving her because of her bipolar tendencies. Bouts of depression would leave her bedridden for months at a time, while manic episodes caused mass cleanouts of their home and furniture to be sold off, only to be rebought three times over.

About a month after he mentioned splitting up, Anne became pregnant with me. Dad stayed. He never wanted children, but he took being a father seriously.

Finally, in their third year together, he caught on to the fact that money was going missing and realized that she had been using him. Soon after he confronted Anne, she left him. Stealing his belongings and emptying his apartment except for his work computer and an empty microwave box to sit on, she fled to Florida, taking me with her. This was when dad met Linda, and they started working together to gain custody of me.

Fast forward a few months – Anne's crimes are getting bigger. After laying low in Florida, she secured a high paying job with a popular computer company near Bakersfield, California. Even with a great job, old habits die hard, and a few months into her new job, she took the company credit card and embezzled $20,000. Unfortunately for Anne, the company she worked for did not take kindly to theft. They pressed charges, and she spent a year in jail before being forced to move to Oregon to find work.

Anne then went on to steal her ex-husband's identity and sink him $10,000 in debt to get by. It only got worse from there.

She met a man named Anthony.

Anthony was an illegal immigrant who worked on a farm in Oregon six months out of the year, living in Mexico when there was no work. He came into the relationship with a busy past; six ex-wives, nine children (one of which he impregnated when she was fourteen), and a few grandchildren. Even so, Anne was smitten.

Anthony encouraged her behavior; he built a house in Mexico to abscond to if she was ever close to being caught. So, she started taking bigger risks.

She stole from stores. Full trailers full of clothing, electronics, and appliances that she could resell for profit. She stole identities. She stole vehicles. There was nothing she couldn't steal, and no one knew how she managed. Every time it seemed that she might get caught, she would flee to Mexico until her feelings of paranoia subsided. After having her fifth child, the second one by Anthony, she finally started slowing down. Until I reached an age that I could help her, that is.

2

BEFORE

I didn't see Anne, often throughout my childhood, but I still knew what she did. After dad earned full custody, she started only picking me up for a visit at Christmas or during the summer, every other year. Sometimes three years would pass without seeing her. I genuinely never knew my biological mother. But I knew she was a criminal. I became so accustomed to her casually stealing on our limited visits, or lying to strangers, that I never thought to tell my parents. By the time I was seven, I knew what hatred felt like. I hated visiting her. I hated that she didn't protect me from her boyfriend, Anthony. I hated the nightmares that came when I slept at her house. I hated feeling like I was going to get arrested and spend life in juvenile detention. I hated Anne.

My feelings only grew stronger once she started involving me in her schemes. The summer before 4th grade, on one of the few visits in my life that Anne showed up for, she masqueraded as a homeless single mother and used me to beg for money.

*****

"Come on quickly. We don't want to miss traffic." Anne ushers me out of the car and through the bustling grocery store parking lot. Even though she has short legs, she moves very quickly, as if she is running from something. I can barely keep up.

We walk through the grocery store door, and Anne takes a sharp right turn to the customer service counter, flagging down the clerk sitting in the office behind the desk. "Good morning! I was just wondering if you had a spare box? I prefer not to use grocery bags; you know how much pollution that plastic causes!"

"Of course, ma'am. Just one?"

Anne nods, and the clerk disappears back into the office. When she returns, there is a large, empty diaper box in her hands.

"Thanks so much!" I stay close on Anne's heels as she walks away from the counter and between two check-out stands, towards the office supply row. We wander up and down the aisles while Anne looks at different things on the shelves. We spend a short time browsing the clothing and housewares as well. Finally, she shakes her head and huffs loudly, "they don't have what we need; let's go." I'm confused, but I follow her out of the store the same way that we came in, without complaint. *I swear she's walking faster than before. I wonder why we still have the box if we didn't buy anything.*

We weave back through the large parking lot towards Anne's beat-up brown sedan. When I try to climb into the backseat, she tells me to wait a minute. I watch as she tears the sides of the box apart until all that's left is a sheet of blank cardboard. She then reaches into her purse and pulls out a Sharpie, still in its packaging. She scribbles something on the cardboard, slips the sharpie back in her bag, and pulls out a brand-new puffy coat. Anne tears the tag off and crinkles the jacket's smooth material up, causing deep wrinkles to appear. "Here, put this on."

Why do I need this? Mild panic sets in. Anne always does weird things on visits, which I ignore for the most part. But I don't want to wear anything that she stole.

I know better than to voice my concerns out loud. I slip my arms into the warm sleeves obediently while Anne picks up her cardboard sheet.

We walk away from the car to the corner of the block, right next to the parking lots driveway. Anne sets her purse behind a bush and holds the makeshift sign up with both hands. I can finally see what she wrote-

OUT OF FUEL, NEED SPARE CHANGE

I didn't know we were out of fuel. I swear she just filled up this morning. I think back hard and picture the fuel gauge. I distinctly remember the needle hovering just under 'F' when we parked at the store.

We stand on the corner for a few minutes before a shiny black SUV pulls up next to us. The window rolls down smoothly, and a middle-aged woman leans out. I can see her patterned leggings and running jacket hugging her thin frame. With her blonde hair in a tight bun, she reminds me of those housewives you see on tv.

"Hey there, do you need help?" She smiles politely at me before addressing Anne.

Anne smiles back, "Yes! I lost my wallet earlier, and we ran out of fuel a couple of hours ago. My name is Anne, and this is my daughter, Alaina."

"Oh, you poor things! It's freezing out there! Here, I want you to take this…" The nice-looking woman digs through her purse before stretching across the passenger seat to hand

Anne a bill and plastic card. "-go get some warm drinks too. Good luck!" She waves and rolls her window up after Anne thanks her.

After we watch the light turn green and the car roll away, I glance over and see that Anne is holding a twenty-dollar bill and a Starbucks gift card. *Do strangers really help people like that? I can't believe what I just saw. I can't believe anyone would fall for Anne's lies.*

I mentally roll my eyes while Anne steps over to her purse and slips the gift inside, then returns to her previous spot and holds up the sign again.

"Aren't we going to go get fuel?" I try my best to sound innocent.

Anne shakes her head, "Not yet. I'm going to see if we can get a bit more cash first."

So much for Anne slowing down on her life of crime.

We stand on the corner for another hour; Anne's story about the fuel and lost wallet changes and becomes more drastic every time someone stops to help. They give everything from a few coins to large bills. Finally, around lunchtime, Anne snaps me out of my thoughts by tugging my sleeve, and I match her brisk pace toward the car again.

Once we are settled into our seats, Anne pulls a large handful of money from her pockets and purse. I sit in the passenger seat quietly while she counts.

"...78, 80, 81, 85!"

"We got eighty-five dollars?" I'm shocked. "I guess that means we have plenty of money for fuel! Should we go and give some back?"

I already know the answer. *You lied to all those nice people.*

Anne laughs, "No, we don't need fuel yet, and this is going to cover us for the next few days."

*****

By the time dad picked me up from that visit, I never wanted to go back.

Unfortunately, the courts don't care about a child's opinion on their parents. I remember writing letter after letter to the attorney and judge, begging to stay with dad full time. I tried explaining that I didn't want to see someone I didn't know, but no one listened. As I got older, I started giving up. Mom told me that when I was 13, the courts would let me make my own choices about seeing Anne. So, I just had to wait. That meant I had to keep dealing with the random visits every few years with a stranger that I thought was crazy. Lucky for me, after she made me stand on the corner with her, Anne skipped out on visits again until the weekend of my twelfth birthday, the summer before 6th grade.

*****

"Hello" I say curtly as I hop into the passenger seat of the car and buckle up.

"Hey Sweetie, how are you doing?" Anne gives me a toothy smile, and the wrinkles in her face deepen. I never realized she was old enough to have such prominent crow's feet.

I want to say, 'Awful since I have to see you…' but, instead, I force my negative thoughts down and mumble, "Fine, how are you?"

Even though I hate having to hang out with Anne and go along with her weird habits, I still enjoy some things about visiting her. She lets me drink coffee and allows me to sit in the passenger seat. I can also text my friends on her phone. Plus, I can pretty much walk anywhere I want in the small town she lives in.

This visit, she apparently has big plans for us. "So, I thought we could go to the French Press, it's a new crepe bar. Then do some shopping at Ross, JCPenney, and Macy's. Tonight, we can go see Transformers after dinner!"

I wonder who's paying. I stifle a laugh and nod. *She must be trying to make up for not coming around the last couple of years.*

We have a calm ride to French Press. Anne asks questions about school here and there. I tried to answer without snapping at her. An awkward forty-five-minute drive later, we pull up to the new café. After some food and a long conversation, I feel a bit warmer towards Anne. She even makes me laugh a few times... until she starts acting weird.

Within minutes of entering the first store on her agenda, our cart is piled high with clothes for me to try on. I put on outfit after outfit in the dressing room, stepping out for her to judge. After every approval, I hand the clothes over the door to her before trying on the next set. At one point, Anne disappears while I re-dress in my own jeans and t-shirt, leaving me to wait in the dressing room for her. After what feels like an hour, she jogs back in, "Hey, kiddo, ready to go?" I nod and follow her out.

Just before we reach the front register, she parks the cart down an aisle and says, "let's go". Confused, I ask, "Aren't we buying anything? Should we put that stuff back?" She shakes her head as we walk through the store's exit. "I already took care of it". I don't say anything, trying to ignore the knot forming in my stomach.

We have almost the same exact routine in the next two stores. Finally, we start heading to her house. Since it's another 30-minute drive, she pulls through a coffee shop drive-thru and buys us both ice-filled drinks. We listen to the radio and have a pleasant chat here and there, but I can't shake the bad feeling that has set in. Even though I have only been with Anne for a few hours, I'm ready to go back to dad's house.

When we finally park in front of her apartment complex, she nearly skips to the back of the car to open the trunk. I gasp in shock. The trunk is full of shopping bags packed tightly with clothes. *How did she get all this without me noticing!* I was with her the whole time except when I was trying on clothes, and I did not see her pay. "Surprise!" She yells out in a sing-song voice.

We carried everything inside and under Anne's supervision, I start dumping the clothing onto the couch and floor. By the time the plastic bags are emptied and crinkled up, half the living room is buried under a massive pile of clothing.

"Happy Birthday, Honey!" Anne nudges my shoulder and grins at me.

I smile weakly while I try to process my feelings. When I start sorting through the pile of colored fabric, eyeing price tags, and adding numbers mentally, my stomach drops. The number keeps grows higher. To anyone that doesn't know Anne, they would see that she just bought her daughter over a thousand dollars' worth of clothing. I know better – *She stole every bit of this.*

At this moment, I decide I will never steal. I'll never be able to get away with it like her, anyway.

*****

23 years later I wonder if Ross stores started using security tags because of Anne. Thankfully, I wasn't exposed to her again for a while. This is where my childhood took a sharp turn for the worst.

3

THE VISIT

I'm sitting on our brown suede couch, legs tucked under my body, with my nose buried in my favorite book. Friday is my last day of eighth grade, and I'm trying to get an early start on my summer reading goal. I lower the book from my face and look up when I hear dad's very heavy footsteps descending the stairs. He walks past the marble-covered bar that separates the kitchen from the living room and stands behind the couch opposite my seat. Mom stops tossing spices into the pot bubbling on the stove and follows him in, perching on a barstool to wait.

"- Yeah, okay, sure. We'll see you Friday then." Dad snaps his cell phone shut and turns to me with a grim look on his face. "That was Anne." My dad shakes his head like he can't believe what he just heard "She wants to pick up for her summer visit on Friday"

No. NO. NO! I jump up from my seat, almost tripping over the coffee table, and yell, "No! I don't want to! Call her back and tell her no!" Tears prickle behind my eyes, and my face starts to burn from anger. I don't want to see her. She hasn't bugged us in two years, and I thought I wouldn't ever have to see her again. A light buzzing starts in my ears while my brain goes into overdrive, trying to think of a way out.

Mom and dad start whispering about possible options as I collapse back onto the couch. It sounds like there's no time to go to court, and I'm going to be forced to spend six weeks with the kleptomaniac liar that is my biological mother. My brain turns fuzzy, and I space out. I have less than three days to prepare mentally.

I'm going to be forced into a tiny space with the person I hate most and two kids under ten that pull at every one of my nerves. She's going to use me to steal again. Or worse, I'm going to have to steal to eat.

I look up and mentally beg the universe - *Please don't let this happen.*

Maybe I can fake being sick. She won't want me if I'm throwing up. Or I bet I could tuck and roll out of the car and run away. No, that's too drastic. Ugh, I hate this.

"Alaina?" *Huh?* I look up from my thoughts and see mom and dad looking at me, concern furrowing their brows. "What are you thinking?"

"I don't want to go!" I blurt out loudly, "I hate being there, you know that, can't we tell her no? I'm 13; I'm supposed to be old enough to decide where I want to stay."

Mom sighs, "Well, the problem isn't the living situation; it's that she has visitation rights. Even if she never shows up. We can't tell her no, or she could turn around and cause a lot of legal trouble for us, and she called so last minute that we don't have time to get in front of a judge to change the order."

I have to roll my eyes. Of course, my parents are more worried about getting in trouble than me feeling comfortable. Sounds like adult talk for 'It's not worth the money'. *Maybe I should tell them about her stealing when I'm there. Or about what Anthony does when she's not around.*

A series of memories creep through my head. Anthony sneaking into my room every visit, telling me that no one will believe me, and if I say anything, I'll get hurt. Anne smacking me across the face when I tried to tell her. A shiver runs down my spine and I decide against saying anything.

"I bet she planned it this way," I say through clenched teeth.

"Oh, I don't doubt that. All we can do is get everything packed up and hope we can change things when you get back after your birthday."

Six weeks. I have to stay there for six long weeks.

Mom and dad never let me swear, but this seems like as good a time as any. "I hate that stupid piece of shit and everyone else there! She's crazy and is just going to ruin my summer!"

Mom purses her lips, obviously not approving of my language, and shakes her head slowly. "I know. We just have to get through this visit."

Dad chuckles at my outburst before making his way through the kitchen and out the back door. Mom starts talking about the pick-up plan for Friday, but I tune out and watch through the window. I have the perfect view as dad pulls out one of his Pall Mall menthols and struggles to light the tip before striking up a conversation with himself.

Have to remember to snag a couple of packs tonight.

I eye his left hand with envy before turning my attention back to mom, who is walking back into the kitchen while she talks. She doesn't know I smoke and certainly doesn't need to find out, so I follow close behind and lean against the counter while she cooks; nodding when her body language cues me to, my thoughts are wrapped in smooth cigarette smoke and mouth filled with the sour taste of resentment.

*****

After two short days and two sleepless nights, Friday's sunrise makes me want to throw up. I've been so sick from stress that I've barely eaten since *the* call.

I walk into school in the morning, tired and in a stupor. As I pass the mural in the middle school's front entry, my eyes slide over the green tree outlines and giant brown and white eagle outlined above a snowy mountain. I stop in my tracks. Seeing the mural puts a small smile on my face while I remember the hours that I spent painting it.

I forgot that this is the last time I'll be at this school. I guess even though I have the worst summer ahead, I should take the time to appreciate my last day of eighth grade. In three months, I'll be across the road at Glencoe High School. *A new student will probably paint over those trees I spent hours on.*

I wander from class to class through the morning, not hearing a word spoken by the teachers. As the day goes on, I start to feel less sorry for myself. By the time that the end of day bell rings, I'm dancing down the hall towards my friends; Jane, Tyson, and Kameron. The trio is stopped in front of my locker. Jane has her phone out snapping pictures of the boys, so I run up and jump onto Kameron's back, just in time for the perfect photobomb. Jane starts giggling, while Kameron spins me in a circle, "FE FI FO FUM!" I snort out a laugh and drop to the floor.

Jane insists that we need pictures to mark the end of our middle school career, so the boys and I line up against the wall. After a few flashes, Jane turns her phone towards me so I can approve the photo. The eyes staring back at me, look haunted. Purple bags boast my lack of sleep. My cheeks are thinner than usual and barely support my fake smile. My dark hair hangs flat around my face; all traces of its normal curls and waves are gone, as if it's been beaten into submission.

I look away after a quick scan. The picture makes me uncomfortable, and I hate looking at myself, even on a good day.

When Tyson and Kameron approve their mugshot style pictures, our group forms a line, and we link arms before walking down the hall. Jane immediately starts making summer plans "So, Tyson is coming over tonight, and it sounds like Kameron will be able to hang out after lacrosse finishes Saturday. What about you, Laney?'

Laney... I have never gotten used to that. According to dad, Indians don't have nicknames or middle names, so hearing Jane call me that always makes me smile. "Ugh, I wish I could hang out... You'll never believe what happened..."

I launch into my story about the awful phone call that came two days prior. Thankfully, my group has known all about Anne since the beginning of our friendship. Kameron shakes his head, Tyson rolls his eyes, and Jane looks like she's scheming "Do you think if you pretended to have the flu, she'd skip it?" I shake my head. "I wish. She's nuts. She probably wouldn't care if I had the plague, as long as she has someone that can carry her extra bag of stolen shit. Plus she knows that my mom and dad hate when she is around." Jane's face drops, and she pouts a little. *Hm... that's an idea.*

"I may be able to get out early. When I was younger, she'd call dad for early pickup if I started causing trouble. I'm thinking I break something or spend every day crying and throwing tantrums. Then I use some reverse psychology and beg to stay after doing something terrible, so that she doesn't catch on, and then boom - I'm home after a week instead of six."

"WAIT, that might actually work!" Jane jumps up and down while she shouts, "Break her computer and anything expensive, you may get to leave the first day!" She laughs gleefully, and the boys and I join in. *I'm going to miss this.*

We wander outside together, towards the soccer field. Like a well-oiled machine, we flop onto the grass, falling together naturally. My feet end up on Kameron's lap, head on Jane's shoulder, and hand in Tyson's. Jane and I agree to keep in contact on Facebook while I'm gone and meet up the day I get back. The boys chat about lacrosse and training over the summer. We're all joking about the teachers we had over the past year when the final bus bell rings. I give Jane and Tyson a quick hug, and they take off for the school. *How are they so excited to get out of here?*

I turn around and notice Kameron is still sitting next to the soccer goal. I grab his attention by dropping down loudly next to him. "What's up?"

He glances at me before looking off in the distance. "I don't know... I'm bummed you're leaving all summer"

I sit up straight and shake my head a bit "Well, it's not all summer, I'll be back before long!"

"It's just that... I was hoping to spend more time with you. Especially without the others."

27

Oh. My stomach flips. "What do you mean? We hang out all the time."

Kameron stands up and holds his hand out to help me. As I rise, he pulls me into his chest and kisses me. I kiss him back, and we stay rooted in place together for a moment. "That's what" He grins down at me, blue eyes warm, and his fingers wrap through mine.

We start walking slowly towards the school. I can feel myself getting angry all over again. Tears are burning, threatening to pour from my eye. I squeeze Kameron's hand and huff, "UGH! It's not fair. Why does she have to show up now?"

When we reach the school's back door, he promises that we'll stay in touch while I'm gone. It's just over a month anyway; he'll wait for me. We share one last kiss before I head towards the pickup area. Dad is already waiting in his usual spot. I hop into the passenger seat and toss my bag into the back, tucking my feet under my body and making myself small. "How was the last day?" I try to answer him, but instead, tears start rushing down my face. In a matter of seconds, I sag into a sobbing mess. "I hate Anne so much!"

Leave it to her to ruin my first kiss.

*****

The last couple of hours at home pass too quickly. I'm tossing the last few things I'll need into my bag when I hear mom tap on my door. "Hey, you almost ready? She's going to be here soon."

"Yeah, I guess. Do you think there's any chance she won't show up, like last Christmas?"

"I'm not sure. She doesn't normally demand a visit like she did this time. I think she's serious."

I nod and pick up my bag, giving my bedroom one last look over. The dark purple accent wall that my headboard leans on glares at me. I've always hated that shade of purple, especially against the pink walls that frame it, but now I would do anything to stay in here.

The doorbell rings, and I ignore it, stepping around my bed to pull a charger from my desk drawer. Running my fingertips along the edge of the desk border, I let myself drift off and remember mom trying to tell me that Santa squeezed this piece of furniture down the chimney seven years before. Mom clears her throat behind me and forces me to come back to the present, so I follow her out of my room.

Seated on my grandfather's antique bench, Anne's broad outline is visible through the muslin curtain that faces the porch. I let out a sigh and try to steady my heartbeat. I give dad a long hug while mom steps around us and opens the door to let me through. She pats my shoulder when I pass, and I shoot her a sad smile. "See you soon, Ma."

When I step outside, Anne stands up. I never realized how short she was before. She smiles wide and reaches up to hug me, the top of her head barely grazing my chin. I roll my eyes and turn away before she can touch me, walking towards her old blue pickup. "Hey, honey, are you excited to get going?"

No. "I wouldn't say excited. You're ruining my summer, you know." I climb into the truck and slam the door. Anne looks appalled. She waddles around the hood and swings the driver's door open wide before clearing her throat and announcing, "Well, excuse me, I have a right to visit you, and I won't deal with any attitude!"

I force a laugh to annoy her. "Well, buckle the eff up, Anne, that's all you're getting from me. If that's a problem, then how about I get out and go back home," emphasizing the last word, I lace my tone with as much venom as possible. Anne's look of shock almost makes having to see her worth it. She freezes in the middle of buckling her seatbelt. "Is this how you talk to Linda and your dad?"

I ignore her question and stare out of the window. *Just tell me to get out of the car. Forfeit the visit. Please.* I'm begging internally while simultaneously trying to think of what will hurt her most. "Of course not. I love them."

"Well, Alaina, I'm your mother, and I love you. So, you need to have a little respect." She starts the car and backs out of the driveway. Mom and dad stand in the window, watching us leave.

I remember something mom said to me once. "Respect is earned, not given." I look at her pointedly. "If you loved me, you wouldn't show up and force me away from my friends and family after years of not seeing you." Anne doesn't say anything. After a couple of tense moments, she reaches to turn the radio on, but the dial is broken. We ride in silence for the hour and a half it takes to reach her apartment.

*****

When the car stops, I snap my head up and look around. We are parked in front of a wire fence, closing off a dark alleyway. The building beyond is a dingy shade of yellow, with doors the color of dirty dishwater. I sigh deeply and step out of the truck, swinging my bag over my shoulder.

Always the creepy places for Anne.

When I step through the gate, I'm even less impressed with the view. Anne's 'front yard' is made up of two square foot slabs of concrete, with a short step up to her front door. I step inside and meet the tiny kitchen first. Hip height counters line both sides of the room, a short fridge stands directly behind the door, with a small sink to its right. On the right side of the kitchen are a miniature stove and a wall of acrylic cabinets that match the blue countertops.

A small, round dining table sits at the end of the right counter, and I flop my stuff on it and scan the rest of the apartment. A back door sits behind the table, and the living room, which is the same size as the kitchen but turned sideways, makes the apartment an awkward L shape. There are two bedrooms to peek into. The first that sits behind the kitchen is packed full of stuff. Floor to ceiling, the walls are lined with shelves, clothes racks, boxes, and various knick-knacks. The second room has two twin-sized beds and no decorations.

I shake my head and quickly take the two strides back to the kitchen to ask Anne where I will sleep. *This place gives off prison vibes.*

"Oh, you'll be on the couch."

I can't hide the annoyance that flickers across my face. "I'm supposed to have my own room, you know. According to the custody agreement."

Anne shrugs. *Obviously, that doesn't matter.*

4

MOVING DAY

The first few days of the visit with Anne are normal by past standards. I do everything I can to avoid her and Quinton and Mercedes, my younger siblings. Luckily, I thought to pack my DS, so I spend most of every day hiding out at the local library, leeching off their internet. Anne does everything she can to spend time with me. Every time I get away from her, I mentally pray that all her failed attempts to bond will push her to send me home. When I was about six, she called dad to pick me up early just because I cried over her boyfriend saying I looked Chinese, so she has to give at some point. But this time is different.

I try to make her life as difficult as possible when I have to be around her. I throw child-like tantrums. I break her dishes. I complain about her cooking. I threaten to call the police if she takes me on a stealing spree. But Anne won't budge.

On my eighth night at her house, I lie on my makeshift bed on the couch and stare at the ceiling. Everyone has long since fallen asleep, but I can't stop my mind from racing.

I wonder what is going on. There's no way she can make it through five more weeks. I'm acting like the worst teenager possible. She would never have dealt with all of this before. Maybe I should call mom and see if she has any ideas.

After an unrestful sleep, I get my answer. Partially.

Anne sits down with her plate of freshly cooked pancakes and yells, "We're moving!" She is beaming at me from across the table. I stare at her blankly and continue to chew. She's obviously waiting for me to say something. "You mean *you're* moving?" I roll my eyes, hoping she catches it.

"Yeah, sure. Anyway, I need all hands on deck today. We have to get this place packed and cleaned up, and we'll be doing a yard sale." I almost choke on my laughter "Why? You don't have anything nice enough to be worth selling." Anne glares daggers at me, and my mouth snaps shut.

I keep quiet as I finish my breakfast and get up to wash the plate. Anne turns around in her chair to face me, and her beady eyes drill a hole in my back. "You know that means you can't run off today kiddo, you're going to help with the kids and packing and –"

I drop the suds covered dish with a loud CLANG into the sink and spin around fast to cut her off. "Excuse me? You can't make me help you. This is supposed to be a 'nice visit with the child you never see' not 'rope a teen into heavy lifting and free babysitting.' I'm not doing anything for you."

I dry my hands and start to head towards the front door, but a hand yanks me by the arm backwards. "Alaina Penelope Franklin! You will do as you're told. You are a *child*, and I am your *parent*! If I say help, you damn will help. Do I make myself clear?"

She sounds like an annoying Pomeranian barking orders, and I cringe at the use of my birth name "Yeah, sure, whatever. I'm going to grab a coffee. Be back soon." I jerk my arm out of her grasp and skulk through the front door.

I damn *well better be caffeinated before I deal with that train wreck.*

*****

When Anne said, 'Yard Sale,' she meant YARD SALE. I stare in shock at the little alley that makes up her front yard. I don't know how she has anything left to move. There are piles upon piles of books, toys, and dishes. Two couches sagging with the weight of blankets frame a dining table stacked high with small appliances. Her tall dresser stands guard over the scene; drawers stuffed too full to open are labelled individually with prices for the clothing inside.

We spent hours sifting through her apartment. The space seems tiny for a two-bedroom, but Anne excelled at packing an entire house worth of stuff into each room. No doubt, it was all stolen. Almost everything she owned was labelled with a price sticker and stuck outside. What remained was packed tightly into a suitcase or small box and stacked into an SUV that her friend dropped off that morning.

Anne handles the transactions as people start buying things. The whole affair begins slowly, with just a neighbor or two wandering around the stacks of old stuff. After a short time, traffic picks up. I eventually have to put down my game and help as people try to hand us wads of cash from every direction. After taking $5 from an old lady, I hear a quiet "excuse me, ma'am" from behind me. I turn and smile at the woman who spoke, "How much for this table," she asks. *Uh...* "That's not for sale, I'm pretty sure we are just using it to hold stuff" Suddenly Anne appears next to me "$25!" She exclaims. *What?*

I step back and watch as Anne sells off the dining table, chairs, and one of the couches to the woman. When she walks past me to scribble down her sale details, I blurt out,

"Why are you selling your furniture? You don't have much, and you won't have any for your new place," Anne shrugs. "There's already furniture at the new house."

House? How can you afford a house? And what kind of place comes pre-furnished... Oh well, if I don't have a couch to sleep on, I guess it's a good reason to get picked up early.

*****

Two short hours later, everything is sold, the car is packed, and the apartment is empty. It somehow looks smaller than when it was inhabited.

"Alright, everyone, load up!" Anne claps her hands enthusiastically and ushers us out of the shell of a home. Quinton and Mercedes climb into the back of the SUV, and I settle into the passenger seat while Anne locks up.

When Anne slams the driver's side door, a stab of pain pokes behind my right eye. An all too familiar migraine is starting. I try to ignore it, but ten minutes after we start driving, the pain hits full force, and I start feeling sick to my stomach. "Hey, do you have any Tylenol?"

Anne gets a funny look on her face, almost like I had read her mind, and she was taken by surprise. "No, sorry, sweetie. But you can take two of these." She rummages through her purse, eyes flicking between the road and her hand. I stare out the window while she drives. Just after we pass a sign reading 'Welcome to Salem,' She pulls out a small, blank, foil packet and hands it to me.

"What is it?" I turn the packet over but can't find a label anywhere. The tablets have an R on one side. "Sort of like condensed caffeine. It should work like Tylenol for pain, but quicker."

I wriggle two of the round yellow pills out and pop them into my mouth, swallowing quickly to avoid any aftertaste. "Hopefully, they work, thanks."

5

ROAD TRIP

Smack. Smack. Smack. *What is that sound? Why are my eyelids so heavy?* Smack. Smack. *My mouth is so dry... Oh.* I realize the smacking sound is my tongue moving in my mouth, courtesy of my brain trying to form moisture. I feel groggy, as if I was woken up in the middle of deep sleep. Or a coma. My head is throbbing worse than ever. My eyelids feel like they each have a ton of bricks on them. The world is spinning.

After three slow minutes of trying to focus and feel half-human, I manage to crack my eyelids open and peer out the passenger window. I catch a glimpse of mountains in the distance before my eyes close forcefully again, and I slump back in the seat.

What a lovely view... It's nice all the buildings moved so we can see them.

Wait.

Something's not right. Where's the city?

I force my eyes open and lurch forward in my seat, spinning around to look through every window in the car. All I can see for miles around is flat land; no city traffic; no streetlights. No giant buildings or apartment complexes. The sky is painted shades of red and pink, and the sun is just barely visible, dipping below the horizon. "Um." I try to speak, but my mouth is so dry I can barely move my tongue. I clear my throat and will my body to work with me. "Um, where are we? This doesn't look like Salem."

Anne pats my knee. "Don't worry. I thought we'd take a little road trip before we get settled."

Don't worry? Well, now I'm worried! "Road trip where? You didn't say anything before. Do mom and dad know? Where even are we?"

Anne purses her lips and fixes both eyes firmly on the road, letting me ramble before answering. "Linda and your father will be fine. We're in California!" My heart starts thudding loudly.

"What! You're not allowed to leave the state with me! What the hell!" Sweat beads on my forehead. This doesn't seem right. *Oh My God. What do I do?* I glance to my right at the passenger door. *Can I unlock the door, or will the auto-lock prevent that? Maybe I could jump and start running.* I look at Anne's purse sitting in the middle console. *Maybe I can grab her phone and call mom before she can stop me? Oh no. Oh no, oh no, oh no.* I have a terrible feeling.

"You are my daughter, and I can take you wherever I want. We are going on this trip as a family, and you *will* behave." She stutters over the word 'trip,' and a knot forms in my stomach. I don't know what it is, but my gut tells me this is all wrong. I can't let her know that I'm uncomfortable.

'Swallow your fear' echoes in my head. I don't know where they came from, but these three words are my mantra now. I

WILL figure out what to do. And the second things go south; I'll run.

*****

We ride in silence for an hour, Anne focused on driving, and the two young kids play on tablets. I sit completely still in my seat, formulating a plan.

I'm too afraid to jump out of the car. We are speeding down the empty highway at 70 miles per hour. Even if I were to survive the jump and not become severely injured, Anne outweighs me by at least 100 pounds and could quickly turn the car around and physically restrain me.

We have to stop for fuel at some point, probably sooner than later, with how big this SUV is. I'll say I have to go to the bathroom and find someone's phone to use. Why couldn't mom and dad give me a phone?

The tension in the car is thick enough to cut with a knife. Of course, Anne can't read thoughts, but it sure feels like it. I finally decide. *I'm going to wait until we get to a rest stop and try to get away then.*

My head is still pounding, so I decide to break the silence to ask, "Do you have anything else to help with my headache? I feel like I'm going to be sick."

Anne pulls the foil pack out of her purse again and hands it to me. "Take two of those." I don't like taking medications I don't know, and these didn't help last time.

As if sensing my hesitation, Anne smiles, "They're cyclical, so after they're in your system awhile, they'll start working. Don't worry. I take them all the time" I guess I don't have much choice. I have to trust her. I pop two of the bitter tablets into my mouth and sit back. It's either drugs or vomit everywhere. *Ha, maybe both at this rate.*

*****

There is a slight pulsing in the back of my skull. I feel like I was run over by a truck. I crack my eyes open and look around. The world is dark outside, only illuminated by stars twinkling in the sky. I grunt with the effort it takes to sit up and force myself to gather my bearings.

We are parked in front of a gas station that features a plaster dinosaur out front, and a faded sign reading 'Welcome to Modesto, California.' The driver's door is open, the seat empty, and the light dinging sound the car makes to let you know the keys have been left in the ignition fills the still air. *Ow.* My head still hurts, although not as bad as before. I turn to look in the back of the car and see that both kids are gone too.

My heart starts racing. *Now's my chance.* I grab my duffle bag and hoodie and nearly topple out of the car. "Okay, Anne, just stay away for a few so I can leave," I whisper under my breath, tying my jacket around my waist. I make my way to the convenience store's front door quickly, trying not to run and draw attention to myself. I barely push the door open when the person in front of me makes me freeze in my tracks.

A tall, gruff-looking man stands at the front counter. He has a bushy beard and small rectangular glasses, short hair that's slicked back, and tattoos covering his bare forearms. Looking at him gives me goosebumps. *Oh no. Oh no. I hope a girl is working here too.* After my experiences with Anthony, I am far too afraid of men to ask for help, especially from one that is two heads taller than me and triple my width. I walk up and down the aisles of the store slowly, praying that I run into a nice girl with a cell phone.

As I turn the last corner, I nearly knock Anne down "Hey! Whatcha doing with your bag, kiddo?" She looks me up and down, and I scramble for words. "Oh, um, I want to change out of my jeans. But I don't know where the bathroom is, and I don't want to talk to the guy. Did you see anyone else?" Anne laughs, "No, they're almost closed, he's the only one here." She motions behind me "Bathroom is there, though, and you don't even need to ask for a key"

"Oh, okay. I'll be right back"

There's no way I can bring myself to talk to the man working, and there's not another soul in this building. *At least Anne doesn't suspect anything.* Something doesn't feel right about this trip, and now I have no way to call mom or dad. A clock above the bathroom entry catches my eye. 10:13. We've been on the road for almost 11 hours, which means I was aslccp for over four hours after each round of 'caffeine pills.' As I walk to the little corner bathroom, I realize something.

I'm trapped.

*****

We've been driving for at least three hours since the rest stop. My body is sore from sitting for so long. My head is still pounding. Anne keeps chattering on like everything is fine. Every couple of hours, she gives me another yellow pill to take, and every pill comes with the promise that it will help once I get into the routine. My brain feels too fuzzy to care anymore. I want to sleep in an actual bed.

I clear my throat to interrupt Anne's latest topic of Spanish music. "Hey, so, where exactly are we going? We have to be near LA or something, right?" My sentence comes out slurred.

"Yeah, we're getting there. We'll stop for the night when we get to Bakersfield."

Wow, way to avoid my question. "What's in Bakersfield?"

Anne starts talking about her great Aunt and other extended family, and I tune out as she drones. *That's not helpful. I can't ask her family for help. But maybe they'll have a phone I can take. At least I know where we are. I have to keep an eye out for an address.* Anne's voice cuts into my thoughts "- We'll be staying at a hotel near there. Just for a few hours so I can recharge before we get back on the road." *Great, I guess I won't be stealing a phone.*

Nearly an hour later, we pull up in front of a seedy-looking motel. The only light on in the two-story building is a flickering bulb in the reception area, with no cover over it. Anne parks right in front of the office and squints through the windshield. "Dang it! They're closed. I guess we're sleeping in the car."

Oh, joy, something else that hasn't changed about visits with Anne. I'm too tired to argue. I'll have to stick a pin in all my feelings until tomorrow. We work together to put the back seats down and clear space the size of a double bed, layering blankets to cushion the area. Once a decent sleeping space has been cleared, Anne settles into the passenger seat while I crawl between Quinton and Mercedes. I pull a spare blanket over myself and ball up a loose jacket to use as a makeshift pillow. The second my eyes close, I'm gone.

*****

"– Big news from New York today, euphoria spreads across the state since a new same-sex marriage law has been passed." A feminine but nasally voice startles me from my sleep. I sit up quickly, nearly ramming my head against the ceiling. Somehow, I turned sideways during the night, and my head was pressed against the door speaker. The kids are already awake and sitting on the other side of the messy makeshift bed. It takes me a moment to adjust to the bright sunlight shining through all the windows. "Jeez, how long was I asleep – What the HELL! Are you INSANE?" I jump forward to look through the front window. The hotel parking lot is nowhere in sight, and we are once again speeding down the highway. "You can't drive with all of us unbuckled!"

"It's fine. We didn't even have seatbelts when I was a kid! Just sit back, we'll stop soon for breakfast, and we can readjust then." Anne smiles reassuringly into her rear-view mirror, which does nothing to settle my nerves.

I hesitate before scooting back and sitting cross-legged next to the kids. *It'd be worse to be between the front seats if we crash.* I try to force my heart back down my throat. *I guess it'll be a good thing if we get pulled over.*

*****

Unfortunately, the universe doesn't do me any favors. We make it another 45 minutes down the road without seeing a single cop. Anne stops at a McDonald's and opens the door for me to get out. I carefully step onto the cracked asphalt with bare feet and start stretching while I look around for a sign to tell me where we are.

LONDON BRIDGE RESORT, LAKE HAVASU, NV

NV?

"Uh, hey, are we in Nevada?"

"Yeah! I thought it could be a fun detour" I shake my head in disbelief. *I shouldn't even be surprised at this point.*

6

FEAR

It's been three days since the garage sale and 12 days since I've seen my parents.

I'm scared.

Anne has dragged us from Northern Oregon, south by 800 miles, through California, and southeast out of Nevada. We are now stopped in Nogales, Arizona. She somehow even managed to get lost and take us halfway into New Mexico. I haven't been able to ask for help anywhere we've stopped. She is either always watching me, or when I *am* alone at a rest stop, the only person to talk to is a scary looking man. I still don't have a straight answer about where we are going, but I have a strong feeling I know now – and I'm afraid it means I'll never see my family again.

She has to be going to Mexico. What was the place she said Anthony lives? Guadalajara? No. That's not right. I wish I'd paid more attention. I hope I could get a message to my mom.

I lose my train of thought when Anne body-slams her suitcase. We finally got to stay in a hotel, and after a long night, we're about to get back on the road. I guess now is as good a time as ever to ask –

"So, Anne," I stutter, clearing my throat. Anne shoots me a dirty look, probably because I used her name. "Is it safe to assume your 'road trip' is to Mexico?" My hands start shaking violently. I'm scared to know the answer.

"Yup! I wanted it to be a surprise. I thought you'd enjoy a tropical vacation"

Tears well up behind my eyes. I'm not sure if I'm about to cry because I'm overwhelmed, angry, sad, or scared.

As I open my mouth to speak again, the shaking from the stress of trying not to cry takes over my whole body. "You can't just take me out of the country without saying anything! That's not fair! Mom and dad have no idea, and I don't want to go! I want to go home." My voice cracks on the word 'home,' and a tear rolls down my cheek.

Anne doesn't say anything. She finishes zipping up her suitcase and exhales deeply before turning to face me. "Honey, your home is with me. Your dad took you from me ten years ago, which was *unfair* to me."

I was supposed to have a great summer before high school started. I should be hanging out with my cousins and friends, not crying in a motel room on the verge of being taken to a foreign country.

I hesitate before asking my next question. I don't want to know the answer. But I need to.

"Are we really only going for a few weeks?"

Anne sighs again and sits on the edge of the bed. "No, Alaina. I feel like it's my turn to raise you. I don't know when we'll go back, if ever, but I plan to keep you until you're 18. If you decide to go back at that point, fine, but I have a feeling you'll love it there and not want to leave."

My heart shatters. Faces flash through my mind. Mom. Dad. My cousins. My Aunt. Kameron. Jane. Every face brings a fresh wave of stinging pain before fading away, taking a small piece of my soul with it.

All the people I love, I'll never see again. I can't hold back the tears anymore. A dark, cold cloud wraps around me, and it takes every bit of willpower I have to avoid collapsing onto the floor and sobbing.

This lady, this monster, that I barely know, just decided to take me away from everything I've ever known.

I got no warning. I was given no choice.

I didn't even get to say goodbye.

A cold wave washes over me, replacing my sadness with fear. *I can't speak Spanish. There are drugs down there. And murder. Anthony will be there. Oh no. I can't be trapped in a house with him.* I want to crawl under the bed and hide as I hid from him when I was a child. *Was this what she was planning all this time that she's been gone? Is this the punishment he told me I'd get for telling anyone?*

Suddenly I feel like screaming. My face flushes with anger. Every lousy memory with Anne fuels a deep rage until I lose control of my thoughts. I want to break something over her head. *Why couldn't she just stay away? I'm going to murder her. I could suffocate her in her sleep. Or stab her with that machete in the trunk. She's not going to get away with this.*

I'm screaming at Anne in my mind, but in reality, I'm frozen in place. I haven't moved an inch. I can't tell if I'm about to drop or run. I feel like I've lost control of my own body while all these new emotions swirl inside me.

It's been three days since the garage sale; twelve days since I've seen my parents.

It will be 1,485 days until I see them again.

I'm terrified.

7

THE PIZZA ANGELS OF HERMOSILLO

I feel numb. I am curled up in the passenger seat of the car with no strength to move, all the feelings gone. All my tears cried out, I can't force myself to open my eyes. *Why would I want to anyway? I'm being driven to my doom. My personal highway to hell.*

After my meltdown in the hotel room, Anne ushered us all out before someone started asking questions. We drove 20 minutes south, stopping before entering Mexico so that border control could check the car for anything illegal. *I'm illegal*, I thought, while they sifted through our belongings. No one questioned the woman taking her three children on vacation.

I should have screamed and ran. I know I should have… But I'm more afraid of the outside world than I am of Anne. Every officer's face that passed by morphed into Anthony's. I was so scared they wouldn't listen, or worse; they'd hurt me like he does. So, I stood silent while they searched, trying to be strong and not just crumple to the ground.

Now, four hours later, we're too far into Mexico for me to even consider running. I have no idea where we are. I don't understand anyone or any signs. I've done a lot of reflecting while we rode in silence. There were so many signs, and I don't know how I missed them. Like four days before we left.

*****

"Hey, can I call mom? She's got a big test tomorrow" I fold the page in my book and look at Anne, waiting for an answer. She rummages through her purse and pulls out her old flip phone, "Sure, just make it quick because I'm almost out of minutes" *Huh, usually, she would say something about calling someone else 'Mom'.*

I quickly dial the number that I've had memorized for seven years and hold my breath while the line rings. Almost three years ago, mom decided to go back to college when my dad started getting sick. Now she is nearly done, and I hate that I am missing one of her final terms.

"Hello?" Mom's voice crackles through the speaker.

"Hey, Ma! I know I'm supposed to be on a visit, but I wanted to call because of your test. How's it going?"

"Oh, good, we're just hanging out over here. I'm ready to go for tomorrow. What's going on there? Are you okay?"

"Yeah, I'm all good. I miss home and wanted to check-in."

We chat for a few minutes before Anne appears next to me, close enough to listen in on the conversation. I glance over and see her tapping on her wrist. I roll my eyes, "Hey mom, I'm sorry, I *apparently* have to get off the phone. I wanted to talk longer."

"That's okay. I'm going to start cooking dinner soon anyway. I'll see you in a few weeks, okay?"

"Yeah! I'll be home soon. –" I'm interrupted by Anne whispering loudly, "Tell her, you love her."

I shake my head at her, confused. *We don't ever say that...*

"Did she just tell you to say you love me?" Suspicion takes over mom's voice.

"Yeah... I don't know why. Anyway, I'll see you later. Tell dad 'hi' for me."

"Alright, let me know if you need anything. Bye." The line clicks and goes dead.

Anne snatches the phone out of my hand. "Why didn't you say you love her? It's going to be a while before you see her again."

I slump back onto the couch. "We just don't say that, and it's only a few weeks. It's fine."

Anne purses her lips and walks away without saying anything else.

*****

I should have known from that conversation. Anne hates mom and would hate hearing that I love her. Why didn't I say anything then? I understand why, though. *I thought I was safe. I would never have suspected that Anne would do something as stupid as...*

Kidnap me?

Is that what this is? It can't be. She has visitation rights.

My heart starts racing. I know the answer, deep down. *I'm being kidnapped.* The story of Kyron Horman surfaces in my mind. I remember how he was supposed to be getting picked up from school by a parent, and next thing, he was just gone. No one had any idea what happened, except that the stepmom did something. Mom called that a kidnapping.

A revelation hits me. *She sold all her unnecessary belongings. She borrowed a car that's not registered to her name. Gave me pills that made me feel weird and sleep for hours at a time. Lied about where we were going so I wouldn't run. And I'm still supposed to be at her house for three more weeks. No one will ever suspect anything until it's too late.*

She's insane. She had to have planned every bit of this.

My numbness is gone now and replaced by something so much worse.

I feel hopeless. *This is it. I'm either going to die or be stuck thousands of miles away from home. Either way, I have next to no chance of ever seeing my family again.*

Mom will go to pick me up in 30 days.

And I'll just be... Gone.

*****

Brrr. That's cold. Where did the heater go? I slowly open my eyes. It's dark out. The car is empty, and Anne left the driver's door open. Startled, I jump out of my seat and grab her door handle to slam it shut. I hit the 'Lock' button three times and crouch back into my seat. Eyes wide, I look around, through all the car windows. We're parked in yet another McDonald's parking lot, but all of the signs are in Spanish this time. I can see a group of Hispanic men standing six feet from the car. My heart starts beating quickly. *No, no, no! This is not happening. Where is Anne? Where are the kids?* I'm watching the group of men so intently that I don't notice another figure walk up to the driver's door.

TAP, TAP, TAP. The knock startles me out of my stillness. I whip my head around to see who is knocking on the window and almost scream from fear. A dark-skinned man is standing there, holding a cloth and bottle of liquid. He must be about 25; muscular, hair cropped short. And smiling? *Do people normally smile at you when they are going to kill you?* I crack the window a couple of centimeters and smile back weakly. His smile widens, "Buenas Noches!" *Oh, I know that. Good evening?*

"Hola, no hablo español…" I stutter out what I think is a sentence, and he laughs. The man starts speaking rapid-fire Spanish. I can barely make out a word, and the now familiar feeling of fear takes over. He holds up the bottle and rag and continues to speak. I'm trying to shake my head and motion that I don't understand, but he keeps shaking the bottle, getting closer to the car. *Is that chloroform or something? Is he going to kill me? Oh no. Anne, where are you?*

For the first time in my life, I want the vile woman to come back. *At least she could translate. Or maybe sit on the guy if he tries to hurt me.* As he starts motioning at the hood of the car, I spot Anne approaching behind him. "Ah! Look! Her!" I try to catch his attention and poin. He finally turns around, and Anne and the strange man start talking. The fear ebbs and is replaced by relief when he waves and starts to walk away. Anne pops open the car door and leans inside. "He was just trying to clean the headlights."

My mind goes blank. "Uh. What?"

Anne starts to explain about people all over Mexico; some try to sell you flowers, some clean your car. All of them are just hoping to make some money.

Well, Toto, I don't think we're in Kansas anymore. I've never seen anyone do something like that in the US. My heart sinks into my stomach. *This is an entirely different place than home.*

Anne starts the car and pulls away from the fast-food parking lot.

*****

It'll be okay. I'll get out of this. Swallow the fear. Have faith. Have faith. Have faith. I keep mentally repeating this to myself, hoping that it will happen if I think it enough times.

I'm drawn out of my thoughts when the car starts to slow down. I look up and see that Anne is pulling into a gas station.

Parking in front of a beat-up looking gas pump, she pulls the key out of the ignition and turns to check on the kids in the backseat. Seeing that they are asleep, she leans in close to me. "I thought we'd be fine until we made it, but I am almost out of money." The smell of bacteria and food build-up from days of not brushing her teeth wafts on the hot breath that comes with her whisper. I nod slowly, trying not to inhale. *Please, please back up.* "I need you to stay here with the kids while I call someone." I nod again, and finally, she moves away and opens her door. I exhale loudly and look at the dashboard clock.

It's been 10 hours since our encounter with the headlight guy. Anne disappears around the side of the convenience store, following a blue sign with an old-fashioned phone graphic on it. *For someone that steals tons of clothes and home stuff, she seems really underprepared to steal a person.*

Twenty minutes pass by, and Anne still hasn't returned. I let out a deep sigh. *I guess we'll be here for a while.* As soon as I reach down into my bag to pull out my book, I hear a muted "Hola! ¿Cómo está?" Turning to my right, I see two men outside my car door, smiling kindly and standing a few feet away. I try to keep my breathing steady. *Alright, this is fine. It's broad daylight; they won't do anything. Have faith. Worst case scenario: I die.*

I roll my window down six inches and smile back, "no hablo español." The taller of the pair steps forward and speaks with a thick accent. "Oh! That is okay. My name is Paul, and this is David" He motions to the shorter man, who smiles and offers a small wave. "Welcome to Hermosillo! We know you have been here for a long time; would you like some food?" *His English is impressive. I didn't think people here spoke any English.*

I let out a sigh of relief and roll the window down further. "Thank you, but I'm sure we'll be fine! We are waiting on a lady that went to use the phone." I pointed in the direction Anne left to. Paul and David smile and nod, almost in unison, and David opens his mouth. "Let us know if we can help at all. We own this place." I nod and smile, and they turn to leave.

For a moment, I contemplate jumping out of the car and begging them to help, only for a moment. Then my fear of strangers creeps back in.

I roll up my window and pick my book back up. Within seconds of finding the page that I left off on, Anne's door swings open, startling me. "Hey, kiddo, I couldn't get a hold of anyone, but these super nice gentlemen are going to help us!" I lean to look around her and see Paul and David standing there. "Uh, okay…" I trail off when I see that her face is covered in red splotches and her eyes are puffy. *Oh. That's a bit dramatic, don't you think, Anne?* It's evident that she's been hiding behind the building crying. Anger starts to rise through my chest. *How can you decide to take someone from their life and not even have the money or resources to follow through? And now you dare to bawl like a baby after you yelled at me for crying over losing my whole family?* I purse my lips and force myself to keep quiet.

Paul walks around the car and pops open the gas tank lid. I hear the distinct click of the fuel pump being pushed into place before liquid starts gurgling through the hose. While Paul fills the car, David walks back into the building, reappearing soon after holding something large and flat. *Is that… pizza?*

Sure enough, as David approaches the car, I can see what he is holding clearly. Two large pizzas, a small bundle of other snacks and napkins, and a full looking envelope on top of the pile. Anne takes the stack from him, looking like she is about to cry again. Parking the boxes in her seat and closing the door, she turns and hugs David. When Paul walks back over, she nearly knocks him over too. The three chat for a few minutes before the men walk away, only turning to wave goodbye.

Once we are back on the highway, I clear my throat. "So, what was all that about?"

"Well, I tried to call a couple of people, and no one could help. Paul came out back to use the phone and saw me crying. I explained the situation to him, and he said he wanted to help because of you kids. Paul and David own that gas station and the pizza place next door, so it didn't cost them much to help us out." As she is talking, I start sifting through the pile of stuff they gave us. After taking stock of the food, I open the envelope. Inside are about 100 blue bills. My eyes widen, and I tune out whatever Anne is saying. *Holy crap. Strangers just gave her a stack of cash! I wonder if this is enough to catch a bus home.* "- almost $200 but in pesos. Plus, of course, food. I told them I'd send them money back because it was too generous."

I look at her, feeling bewildered. "Did you say they gave you $200? So, you run out of money while taking me from home, and somehow get help from... what? Pizza Angels?"

She is either a master manipulator, or the universe hates me enough to help her. Maybe both.

8

EL COLOMO

"We're here!" I look up from my book when Anne yells out loud and I nearly have a heart attack. We are driving over a very narrow concrete bridge with no railings. I peek out of the window and see that there is barely three inches of extra space on either side of the large SUV, and a 20-foot drop below. *Breathe. It'll be okay.* I try to steady my heart rate. After a very long 30 seconds, we make it to solid ground again, and I get a chance to look around properly.

There are no signs. No big stores. Nothing to tell me where we are. "Where is 'here'?"

Anne smiles wide, "El Colomo! Only the best town in Mexico" *Wow. Either the rest of this country is a shithole, or she has low standards.*

All the buildings we creep past are clearly older than her. With colorful paint peeling off, it reminds me of an abandoned clown town. All the buildings are made from concrete blocks; all the windows have bars on them. *Maybe clown jail.* As I take in what I'm looking at, I notice most people walk around instead of driving.

As if Anne knows what I'm thinking, she starts pointing and explaining, "The great thing about this place is that it's small enough to walk everywhere, most people never drive. Over there" she motions to our right, and I turn to see a sizeable stone-paved square. There is a fountain in the middle and a few people sitting against a short wall around the edge. Behind the square is a large building with stained glass windows and a large arched doorway accented with hibiscus bushes. "That is The Plaza, that's where all our festivals are held, and sometimes small markets" She emphasizes the 'z' in "plaza," making it sound like an 's', and a mild Spanish accent follows in the rest of her words. *Why do you sound like that? You're white as anyone could get.*

Anne turns the car left, and we start driving up a steep hill "I'll take you through the rest of town later. This is the road we live on. Over there is a tortilla maker. There is the best vegetable stand in town, and up there on the left is a grocery shop" My eyes follow as she points around, trying to soak in everything she is telling me. Maybe when I learn some Spanish one of these people can help me.

We finally reach Anne's house. She turns right, into a dirt driveway. There is a tall concrete wall on the opposite side of the yard, with a massive stack of concrete blocks to the left. Anne pulls around in the small paddock and parks in front of a clothesline. The plain grey house is to our left, and my stomach drops a bit when I see a beat-up looking green truck next to us. "Is Anthony here?" I stutter as fear starts to set in again. Anne shakes her head "No, he'll be staying to work in Oregon for a few more months. That's our truck" *Oh, thank God. I hope I can get out of here before he comes back.*

Anne gets out of the car and motions for me to follow. Every step I take toward the house feels like a step further away from home.

Once inside, I realize that 'house' is a generous term. The heavy iron door opens to a large, bare room. On the right is a small kitchen, separated from the rest of the room by a concrete bar counter. On the same wall as the front door is an expansive window that opens to what looks like a hot tub made of cement, without any jets or electronics. On the back wall are a stove, a counter, and a fridge.

The room we enter is the length of two standard bedrooms and only holds a plastic table and chairs. At the back of the left side of the room is a cut-out door, with a curtain hanging in front of it. Anne walks up behind me. "That's the bathroom, there's no hot water because Colomo functions off rainwater, but we have a basin for baths if we heat water on the stove." I nod in shock. This is unlike any house I've ever seen.

"The kitchen doesn't have a sink; we use the pila" She motions at the thing that I thought was a non-functional hot tub. "And the microwave has to be moved to use it." I nod again and walk across the room through another cut-out doorway. There is a small step up from the main room's rough gravel-like floor and onto smooth concrete. *Jeez, this place is like a grey washed jail.* The room I step into is also bare. There is another heavy iron door on the back wall, flanked by two windows with iron bars. To the left is a doorway, which Anne explains is her room, the entrance to the right is my room, to share with the kids. I walk in to see a makeshift hanging rack for clothes. Upon closer inspection, it is clear that the rack is made from a recycled broom handle, hung from an exposed beam with plastic orange rope. On one side of the room is a mattress on top of a plywood piece and propped on two sawhorses.

On the other side of the room is a double bed with a standard frame. Anne walks past me to set some bags on the larger bed and claps her hands together. "Welcome home, kiddo!"

My stomach drops, and my breakfast threatens to come back up. *There's no way this is ever going to be home.*

*****

It takes us a few days to get the car unloaded. My clothes still sit in the dusty polka-dot duffle bag, even though Anne insists I should put them away. I feel so uncomfortable in this new place; I don't know what to do with myself, so I find a spot on the floor in the middle room and leave a pillow propped against the wall and a stack of books next to it—my makeshift personal library. The kid's toys make the house a little livelier, but it still gives me weird jail vibes. *Which is fitting considering I'm a prisoner.*

9

DIRT

It's been seventeen days since I last saw my family; ten days since I spoke to mom, nine days since we left Oregon, and five days since we met the Pizza Angels.

Who knew nine days could feel like more than a year. *There are still 25 days until mom will drive up to Anne's empty apartment, expecting to pick me up.* Thinking about this hurts my heart. I thought heartbreak always came from a bad relationship. I never realized I could feel so crushed from anything else.

I'm sitting in a hammock, my eyes glued to a page in my book, but I can't make myself read. Almost every day since we arrived has been spent like this. I pretend to read while feeling like I'm having an existential crisis. The kids disappear into town to play from sunrise to sundown. And Anne cleans. Yesterday, Anne must have gotten tired of me sitting in the middle of the floor, and she hung up my new seat in the middle of the room. *At least if I die here, I'll be easy to bury. Just wrap me up in the hammock and call it a day.* I smile a bit to myself. Grotesque humor isn't my thing, but it's now keeping me going.

I give up on trying to read and lean back to stare at the dull grey ceiling. Between the concrete block walls, concrete floors and ceilings, bars covering the windows, and heavy iron doors, I feel like this could be the perfect setting for a prison-based show. I let my thoughts drift away, imagining a TV crew and screenplay writers hustling around. Before long, I realize that the house is eerily quiet. *Guess I was left here...*

I climb out of the hammock and stretch, my fingertips almost reaching the ceiling. *I guess today is as good as any to try and explore.* I walk into the bedroom I sleep in. It's already a small room, but Anne added a couple of plastic drawer stands and a small table into the mix, and now it feels like a broom closet. *This is probably still a downgrade to Harry Potter.* I flop onto the double bed that I share with Mercedes and feel around under a pillow until I find my DS. I flip the screen open and check if there's any internet available. I've been checking at least five times a day since we arrived, but still no luck. *I wonder if Anne knows this works on WIFI? Ha, she'd probably snatch it, if so.*

I sigh deeply and hide my treasure again before heading for the door. It's brighter outside than I expected. I'm trying to look around and can't help but squint. *It's like the sun burns ten times brighter here than at home.* I take a few steps further into the light. It feels strange being outside for the first time in five days. *Alright, remember the steps. 2, 3, 4, right, 2, 3, right again.* I start counting and keeping track of the turns I make, so that I don't get lost.

A few minutes after leaving the house, I find my way to the corner store we passed on the drive. I don't have any money, but I figure I should check out the inside anyway. I hesitate, then step through the small painted archway into a building the size of my living room at dad's house. To the left of the door are two large coke coolers, filled with milk, sour cream, cheese, and other dairy. To the right is a display stand with chips, cookies, and plastic-wrapped snacks. Fruits and vegetables line the walls, and directly in front of me is a checkout counter.

A short, old-looking woman sits behind the bench. When I walk in, she looks up and smiles without saying anything. I smile back before slowly walking around the room. My eyes land on snack after snack, seeing nothing familiar. *No strawberries? No donuts? And what on earth is 'pan'?* I look up when I hear a creaky 'Necesitas ayuda?' *Shit, what's that mean?* "Um, no hablo español…" I trail off, hoping my only Spanish sentence sounds correct. I feel silly for being in a Spanish speaking country and not being able to understand anything. *Well, it's not my fault anyway. Maybe if I could tell the future, I would have paid attention in Spanish class.*

The woman nods, smiles again, and picks something up from behind the counter, slowly walking over to me. She gently takes my hand and places a small foil bag in my palm, and in heavily accented English, says, "For you". I look down at the bag and tears start to form. "Cheetos! Gracias". *At least I can say thank you.*

I wander out of the tiny store and start walking down the road, my heart heavy all over again. *Who knew something as small as a bag of chips could make me feel emotional?*

It's not the chips… It's a small piece of home. And the fact it came from a stranger, for free. I find a patch of dirt between buildings where there's no fence and sit down, allowing the puff of dust that kicks up to settle before I tear open the small pouch full of crunchy snacks. The familiar smell of powdered cheese fills my nose and overwhelms me. Within seconds I pull my knees in and let tears flow freely. *I want to go home.*

Part Two

10

THE CITY

"Hola Sofia, ¿cómo está? I give the shop owner a wave as I walk past. I hear the kind old woman call after me, "Quieres pan o chocolate? ¡Tengo mucho mas!". I turn and laugh. "Gracias, pero no. Yo voy a comer desayuno ahora" *Who knew that after two months I would be able to understand and speak back. 'How are you, do want bread or chocolate?' I have too much. No, thank you, I'm going to eat breakfast now.*

It's been sixty-six days since we arrived in Mexico. The first couple of weeks were brutal. I cried a lot. After our third week here, I realized that crying and feeling sorry for myself wasn't going to get me home.

I started going on walks every day, meeting locals, and trying to learn some Spanish. Thankfully, most people were nice and helpful. I was uneasy at first, but I realized that the more I was out, the more that people would recognize me, and the less likely it was that I would get hurt.

I woke up with the sun every day, even weekends, and sat in my hammock to read. I only brought a couple of my Harry Potter books with me, but I kept reading them repeatedly. Dumbledore had a surprising amount of wisdom to share.

After reading for an hour or so, I'd eat breakfast and then go out on a walk. I finally got to a point where I had a mental map of El Colomo. I knew exactly where to go to swim, the best places to get lunch, and I had a list of all the places I wanted to draw.

I'd often spend hours by the river through the day, writing lists in the dirt. *No one could possibly know what I'm planning if it disappears when I walk over it.* I thought my logic was sound. I would sit on the riverbank and try to figure out how much it would cost to get home. Coming up with plans to work here and there, I also kept a backup plan of just stealing the money I needed. I wasn't a thief, but this was life or death. *At least, it feels like it.*

But, today, as I walked past Sofia's store, I couldn't help but forget all my scheming and potential plans to steal.

Today I'd have my first chance in months to get a hold of my parents.

Today, Anne is taking me to the city.

*****

Come on, time. Hurry up. I'm sitting in one of the plastic chairs in the dining room, waiting. After a quick breakfast, Anne said we'd be going in twenty minutes. I swear the clock slowed down then.

Finally, I watch the second hand click over the large number ten, and I jump up from my seat. "Guys! Are we going?!" I can't help but contain my excitement. I have a small backpack packed with my DS, a book, and some snacks. *If there's an opportunity to run, I'm taking it.*

Anne appears in the doorway and laughs "Alright, eager beaver, let's go!"

*****

Even though I didn't choose to be here, I must admit that this place is amazing. We're driving down a four-lane road, and buildings tower over us on either side. Palm trees line every sidewalk, and the deep blue ocean, framed by white sand, peeks through long alleyways cast in shadows.

A few kilometers into the city, the tall office type structures morph into smaller, stucco-covered shops and houses. The buildings are all bright and clean, covered in earth tones, and they look like they've been standing for a hundred years. People of all colors mill around through the neighborhood. I can't tear my eyes away from the beauty of history until we drive down a side road and emerge back into the midst of new, stuffy looking towers. The large windows that line every available surface reflect hot sunlight into my eyes, forcing a headache to form.

"We just drove through *El Milicon.* Like the historic district," Anne smiles at the look of awe on my face and continues pointing at various buildings as we pass them, telling me where things are. There's no way I'll remember it, but I still listen intently.

After twenty minutes of weaving up and down the busy city streets, we pull into an underground parking garage. Anne turns and looks at me, grinning. "You ready?" I smile back and nod. She's excited because she thinks I've accepted this life. I'm excited because I'm about to get a hold of my mom. My whole body shakes and my palms are clammy. *Get ready, Anne, you're going down.*

*****

69

Come on, internet. Let's go! It's been forty minutes since we walked into the mall, and all my attempts to sneakily hop on the internet from my DS have failed. The old game system doesn't process quickly, and by the time I can pull up the menu to find a connection, Anne is moving to the next spot.

My fifth attempt is my last, as she finally turns around and notices, "Put that thing away! We're supposed to be out for fun, not playing games. You can play at lunch" Okay. *That's only in an hour. I can wait.*

Waiting is so difficult. The seconds feel like hours, and as they creep by, the minutes feel like days. We are just leaving a kid's clothing shop when Anne announces lunch.

We trudge up the stairs to the second level of the mall and come face to face with a McDonald's.

I almost laugh out loud from the irony. *Why is every big moment in my life marked by McDees?*

After we order and sit down, I set my DS on the table loudly and look at Anne. She rolls her eyes and finally tells me I can play.

I whip the lid open and click-through settings as fast as possible. After four long minutes, I get a stable internet connection. I could cry from relief.

I scroll through the main menu, squinting at the small view screen until I find it. I click on the 'WWW' icon and exhale.

My thoughts are racing, and my heart is pounding while watching the small blue loading bar move from left to right. It stops at 95% for a few moments, and I wait with bated breath, scared that any movement will keep it from working.

100%. The screen fills with blue-colored pixels, and I click and scroll to find a precious message thread – Linda Davis. Mom. Relief floods over me and it takes everything in me to hold back my tears. Possible unread messages fly through my mind 'I miss you' 'Where are you' 'Please come home.'

I click on mom's name to bring up a chat bubble.

No. There's no way. Come on. Something isn't loading.

My heart sinks.

'LINDA DAVIS: COME PLAY FARMVILLE WITH ME!'

Message received May 13th, 2011

I start clicking through message threads and profiles furiously, pleading with the universe for something to come up. Chat after chat, I see there's no new messages. Not a single person has tried to get a hold of me.

Sixty-six days. Sixty-six since Anne took me from my home.

I've been gone since fucking June.

And no one cares.

I no longer feel like I'm going to cry from relief. My emotions swirl into a ball, morphing into something new.

Despair.

11

DEPRESSION

We have a quiet ride from Nuevo Vallarta to El Colomo. I haven't told Anne what I was doing, or why I'm upset. *Best to process on my own. I'll tell her soon. I'll have to, since I'm stuck with her.*

I spent the entire thirty-minute lunch scrolling and trying to find some sort of lifeline from family or friends. I had one email, and it was from Jane telling me that Kameron got a new girlfriend. *As if that's important now.*

I thought about writing to mom. I couldn't figure out what to say. *'Hey, I know you don't care, but I'm stranded in Mexico and could use some help'?* or *'Please come get me, Anne took me, and I'm scared'?* Maybe, *'I'll try to pay you 10 thousand dollars if you can just send me a bus ticket'.* No matter what feeble plea developed from my thoughts, I couldn't make myself type anything into the little blinking chat box. I didn't know how to put my feelings into words, and I feared what I may get back in response. Or, even worse, if no response came at all.

Maybe I'll try again another day.

Anne pulls back up to her gloomy box of a house, and I make my feet shuffle inside. Flopping into my hammock, I glance at my book and then lie back. *The trio can wait. I need to sleep.*

So that's what I do.

*****

For almost two weeks, I only leave my cocoon to use the restroom and scavenge for snacks. I can feel myself spiraling further into a depression every day, but I don't have the energy to try to climb out.

The lack of communication from family hits me harder with every day that passes. I can't fathom why no one would reach out if they miss me.

So, I sleep. And I sleep. And I sleep.

Until, one day, Anne decides that I'm not allowed to sleep anymore.

"Come on, get up!" Her loud voice cuts through my eardrums. I roll over and ignore her.

"Let's go, Alaina. You're done sulking around. I don't know what's going on, but we are getting you out of the house."

I open my mouth to speak, and my voice cracks. "No, my head hurts, and I'm tired."

Anne yanks the blanket from my body and pulls one side of the hammock up until I'm eye-level. "You are not tired. You're lying around feeling sorry for yourself. Let's go."

Ugh. I drag myself out of the fetal position. As soon as both feet are on the ground, the room starts spinning, and a loud, heavy pulsing starts behind my eye.

Anne takes my hand and pulls me through the house to the dining room table. Moments after I slump into a chair, a plate piled high with steaming food is placed in front of me. My stomach shrinks in and growls loudly. *When was the last time I ate?* I pick up the fork in front of me and start shoveling rice into my mouth.

After the plate is clear, Anne sits down. "Sweetie, I'm worried. What's going on?" *Ugh, don't sweetie me.*

I breath in and force my mouth to move. "When we went to the mall, I used the internet. I tried to get in contact with mom and dad." My lip starts to quiver, and tears threaten to spill. "I didn't have a single message from anyone. It's like I disappeared, and no one cares and-"

Suddenly Anne picks up the plate in front of me and throws it at the table, causing a loud shattering sound to crack through the air. As ceramic pieces fly around us, Anne yells, "Why would you do that!"

I cringe hard and cold fear starts spreading through my body. "I miss them. I at least want them to know I'm safe…" My voice is shaking as I trail off. Anne breaths deeply for a moment, then nods slowly.

"I see. Well, I'm sorry you didn't see what you wanted. Maybe this is a sign that you're where you're supposed to be?"

"Yeah, maybe." My heart sinks, and I feel like throwing up. *This can't be the rest of my life. I shouldn't be stuck in a tiny depressing house, sharing a room with two other kids. Eighth grade can't be the last of my education.*

Anne interrupts my thoughts by placing her hand over mine. "It will get easier. I had a hard adjustment the first time I moved here too. Why don't you go read outside and try to relax?"

I nod and push myself out of the hard plastic chair. *Why does she make it sound like I chose to be here?*

After I have my current read safe in hand, I head out to find a padded patch of grass under a towering tamarind tree. *Alright, universe, give me some wisdom.*

I open my book to the last page I folded down. The first words my eyes land on make my heart skip a beat –

'Fight, and fight again, and keep fighting, for only then could evil be kept at bay.'

Oh.

*****

Two hours pass before I looked up from my book. The sun has started dipping down, and the air has a chill to it that warns me, night is coming.

I stand up and stretch deeply. Anne was right; I needed to read. I realized something while I was sitting alone. *The only way I'm going to get where I want to be is to use the resources at hand.*

Mom and dad may not want me, but I'm sure I can find someone to stay with back home, so I'm going to be nice to Anne. The less she suspects, the better.

I wander into the house and see Anne setting a large dish on the table. I pull over a chair and start serving the chayote stir fry in front of me. Once we are all settled in and eating, I clear my throat. "So, I was thinking. You're right; maybe I am supposed to be here." Anne lowers her fork and beams at me. "I'm so glad you think so! I think this will be great in the long run."

I nod and smile before tucking back into my dinner.

12

MOM

Anne pulls the rusty old truck into a large parking lot, and I look around. There is a huge white and grey building on one end of the lot, it's topped with a dome, and I can see the fin of a plane peeking over the edge. Tall white pillars line the sidewalk in front of the building, banners hanging from them with photos of planes and luggage.

"What are we doing here?" Words leave my mouth slowly, and I realize how heavy I feel.

"We're going shopping!" I look around again and back at Anne, confused beyond belief. "Is this an airport?"

She nods and points to one end of the building. "There's a shop in there that we're going to visit."

Oh, okay. I sit back in my seat while Anne finds a parking spot.

Once parked a short walk away, we start for the entrance to the airport. I stop in my tracks when I realize it's just Anne and me. "Where are the kids?" My words are still slow, and I can't shake the fog that clouds my brain. Anne takes my hand and pulls me back into stride. "They stayed home, remember? It's fine."

I don't remember, but I keep following obediently.

Before I know it, we are standing inside a small shop with no windows. I can't explain how we got here so fast, but it was almost like how you move in a dream. Anne and I walk by the shelves and stacks of books and clothing; this is such a strange store. They have everything, but also nothing at all.

I round a large pile of books, trying to read the spines. My eyes can't focus on the words. As I'm about to give up, something moves in my peripheral vision. I glance up and see the back of a tall, broad figure, clad in a black coat with short unkempt graying hair sticking out. My heart skips a beat. *I swear that could be dad.* My eyes slide away from the eerily familiar silhouette and land on a smaller feminine frame next to it. This one is wrapped in a dark brown peacoat, with blond hair just brushing the collar. Bright pink stripes on one side of the straight locks startle me, and before I can stop myself, I yell, "Mom?" The two figures turn and face me, and I can see clearly – It *is* my parents. At the same moment, I am being pulled from the store. Anne is yanking me, yelling, "Come on," which I can barely make out over the ringing in my ears.

As Anne pulls, my parents follow. They are just far enough behind us that I can't reach them, but close enough that I can see every detail of their outfits.

Mom is wearing a white sleeveless shirt with brown spots on it, her brown peacoat, and a pair of blue and brown shoes. Her hair is done up Christmas style, with pink streaks to mimic a candy cane. Dad is wearing a typical green flannel and worn-out jeans, with blue Velcro shoes. His puffy black coat with extra pockets is zipped halfway, and his hair obviously hasn't been brushed in weeks.

I feel tears well up. I want to stop and run to them, but Anne won't let go of me. It's like she's suddenly developed superhuman strength. We jog through the airport, around people with blurred faces, and towards a massive staircase. *I didn't know this place had stairs. I thought it was one floor.*

Anne pulls me up a short set of steps, and I turn to see my parents still close behind us. We start up a full flight of stairs, and I peek over the rail. Mom and dad have stopped at the bottom and are looking up. Mom is yelling something, but I can't make it out.

Up another flight of stairs, my parents finally follow.

As we climb higher and higher, they stay exactly one floor below us. Tears are flowing down my face. I can't breathe. *They're so close. Why can't Anne slow down?*

I try to take a breath in, and it feels like there's something on my face. I scratch at the invisible barrier, and I realize it feels soft.

Oh.

*****

My eyes open slowly, and I pull the pillow away from my nose, gasping for air. I've tossed and turned so much in my sleep that my blanket is gone, and my head is resting in a divet left from a popped spring in the mattress. I sit up in bed and put my hands on my face. My cheeks are wet with the tears I cried while I slept. The image of mom and dad chasing me starts to fade as the fog finally lifts.

I pull my knees up and hug myself, letting tears flow freely. Reality hits. *It was just a dream. A cruel, hope-filled dream.*

13

SCHOOL

"What do you think of trying the school here?" Anne's question snaps me out of my thoughts. I've been replaying my dream in my head repeatedly. I feel like I'm going mad. It felt so real.

I look at Anne with a blank expression. Her words didn't process for some reason. After a moment, she asks again. "Oh... Yeah, that would be nice. I'm supposed to start high school next week."

"That's what I was thinking. If you want to try, we can get you enrolled in the school here. You go early in the morning; you'd walk down with the group of kids in your class and then be home for lunch." I chew slowly while I contemplate this. That means I may be able to pick up more Spanish, plus maybe find someone that would understand that I shouldn't be here. "Sure, let's do it."

Anne claps her hands together and beams, "Great! I'll get your uniforms organized!"

Um… Uniforms?

*****

A few days after I agreed to go to school, I'm sitting at the dining table yet again. This time, Anne says she has a surprise for me. She struggles to bend over and pull a mass of pink fabric from a plastic grocery bag. She flops the wad on the table, and it reminds me of already chewed pile of bubble-gum. I reach out and pick up the woven cloth for a better look. It's a sleeveless dress, with a zippered pocket on each side, and double-layered, so it's thick. "What do you think?" Anne is waiting anxiously for my answer.

"Well... It's something..." I trail off and keep inspecting the dress. Anne chuckles and picks up another dress that looks the same. "These are the school uniforms!"

"Ohhhhh. Thank god, I thought you were trying to give these to me as a gift. They're awful and look like the Pepto-Bismol man threw up on them!" I'm laughing at my own joke so hard I don't notice Anne set a pair of black Mary Janes and white stockings on the table. My laugh stops, and my face turns to stone. "Wait, you're serious? Do I have to wear all this? I hate dresses. Can't I wear pants?"

Anne shakes her head. "No, the dress code is strict. After age 10, girls wear dresses and boys wear pants."

"That is some sexist bullshit. What if I wear pants anyway? They can't do anything."

"No! Don't do that. One girl tried last year because her brother ruined all her dresses. She got a flogging and sent to another school. You don't have to commit to this; just try it out."

Jesus, is this a Catholic school? "Alright, sure."

*****

81

"Come on, Alaina, wake up" I crack my eyelids open and try to see what's going on. Anne is standing over me, moonlight outlining her frame. I rub the crusty sleep from my eyes and sit up. "Come on, kiddo, you have to get ready for school."

"What time is it?" I look around and see that both kids are still asleep. "Five. School starts in an hour."

Ugh. I flop back down on my pillow and huff loudly before rolling out of bed. Ten short minutes later, I'm fully dressed in my new pink dress. "I look how I feel now – like barf." My half-hearted joke falls on deaf ears as Anne juggles cooking eggs and slicing *pan* for my breakfast.

Thirty minutes later, I'm standing in front of the house, waiting for a group of girls to walk past. They round the corner, and I follow, staying about ten paces behind. I'm thankful some people know the way, but I'm not about to try to talk to them.

The girls lead me down the hill, right through the plaza, across the narrow bridge with no rails, and through a path lined with Tamarind trees. Twenty minutes into our walk, we approach a large courtyard, the size of two basketball courts put together. White buildings line every side of the area, and I can see different aged kids walking into each building. I follow the girls into the room closest to us and find a desk at the back.

It seems like a typical classroom. The kids are all playing, throwing stuff around, and laughing, until the teacher walks in. "¡Buenos días, niños y niñas!" The class calls back in unison, "Buenos dias, Maestra Maria," before uniformly standing and facing the front.

An intercom speaker in the corner crackles to life, and a man's voice filters through. Between the fast speaking and static, I can't make out what he's saying, so I stand and strain my ears, hoping to catch a snippet. After a couple of minutes, the class says "Gracias" together and sits back down. The teacher starts speaking, and I realize that I can barely understand three words of every sentence. I look around and wait for cues from other kids. Soon after class starts, everyone reaches into their desk and pulls out a green bound workbook. I follow suit and open to the middle of the book. *Oh! It's math!* I can understand math, no matter what language. I pull a pencil from my bag and get to work. After scribbling out a few answers, I realize - *I know all this.*

I start flipping through the book, as I get to the end, confusion sets in. It's full of fractions and multiplication. I finished this type of math in fourth and fifth grade. I should be starting Geometry or Algebra 2 this year; *this is kid stuff.* I sigh and complete the page I was working on. The bell rings, and kids start shuffling around, putting books back in their desks, and walking out through the door. I follow and watch as groups of kids start forming, and friends start playing games. It must be break time. I look around and don't see anyone I know, so I make my way back to the classroom and cross my fingers that Maestra Maria can speak English.

"Hello, miss?" I trail off and wait. Maria sets her pen down and smiles, "Si?" *Dang, it.*

I try to piece together a sentence that roughly translates to "I don't belong here," and the woman's smile falls, a bewildered look forming. She speaks in heavily accented English. "What do you mean?" "Oh, I'm so glad you speak English! I'm trying to say I'm in the wrong class. I should be going into year nine, but these lessons seem like year five or six." Maria nods and stands, motioning for me to follow her.

We walk out through the courtyard together and into a small building that I didn't see before. It's painted blue and just has one room in it. We walk through the iron-framed doorway, and Maria speaks to a large man sitting behind the desk. He looks puzzled before asking me, "How old are you?"

"I'm fourteen. I'm not sure about here, but in the US, fourteen is in year nine..." The man lets out a deep belly laugh and stands. "Maria teaches twelve and thirteen. You go to Escuela Secondaria!" I smile, but can't hide the confusion on my face. The man searches for the words and offers, "Second school? High School?"

"Yeah! That's it!"

Maria and the nice man chat for another minute before she leads me back to the classroom. I wait at her desk while she scribbles a note and hands it to me, "You give that to your mom." She smiles, and I thank her. Grabbing my bag, I start walking back the way I came in just an hour before.

So much for school. I laugh out loud as I walk. Who knew High School could mean different things in different countries?

14

SAN SEBASTIAN AND TEPIC

Eighty-eight days have passed. I'm really starting to enjoy the little town of El Colomo. The locals are friendly and strike up a conversation whenever I walk around town. *It's going to be a shame when I leave. Maybe I'll come back here to vacation when I'm older.*

I'm sitting in the plaza on one of the many brick ledges when Anne approaches, Mercedes in tow. "Hey, monkey!" Mercedes scales my back and lets out a strange hooting sound, which I assume is her imitation of a primate. I raise my hand to block the sun and look at Anne. "What's up?"

She smiles back at me and sits before speaking, "So, we have a little extra money left from what Anthony sent this week. What do you think of seeing Guadalajara? We could go through Tepic, San Sebastian, then stay in Guadalajara before we come home."

I think for a moment, trying to piece together where these places could be. Having no idea, I nod instead. "Yeah, that could be fun."

Anne is positively beaming, "Great! I'll get everything ready!"

*****

It is incredible just how much of my life has been spent in a car.

Two short days after Anne presented the idea, we're on the road to a new city, the small truck packed with everything we could need for a week. The kids opted to ride in the truck bed, which makes me queasy. As we ride the shoulder of winding roads with steep drop-offs, I can't help but imagine us toppling over the edge.

Our three-hour drive is filled with singing and storytelling until, eventually, Anne and I get to the point of reminiscing. Our conversation starts light-hearted and fun. "Do you remember the time you stayed with Auntie Lynn?" Anne asks, smothering a chuckle. I smile, remembering my tenth birthday with her sister fondly.

*****

Ding dong. I wait anxiously in front of a maroon-colored door, bouncing on the balls of my feet. After ten long seconds, I hear the lock click, and the door swings wide open to reveal my Aunt Lynn. I've been so excited about this visit. Anne couldn't make it to her weekend with me, again, so Lynn said I could stay the night with her.

I grin wide and wrap my arms around my aunt. She's short, standing just under five feet, and her shoulder-length grey hair makes her appear older than she is. "Hi, sweetie! It's so good to see you" Lynn's warm voice reminds me of honey and feels like home.

As much as I don't like seeing Anne, Lynn will always hold a special place in my heart.

I follow the small woman into her kitchen and set my bag down on the floor. Lynn wraps me in a tight hug, "Oh, you crazy kid, I've missed you!"

I giggle and squeeze back. We chat for a few minutes before Lynn jumps, startling me. "Oh, my goodness, you must be hungry! Do you want some banana bread? Or a sandwich? I may have some snacks in the pantry too!" I laugh, "It's okay, Auntie, thank you. I can wait for dinner." I beam at Lynn, and she hugs me again.

Just a few hours later, we've finished dinner and are sitting in the living room talking. Auntie Lynn always talks to me like an adult. It's a nice change from home.

"Oh!" She gasps. "Do you want to watch a movie? I just got Braveheart on DVD, and I have leftover pie!" She wiggles her eyebrows at me, causing me to laugh loudly.

"Can we make a fort for it?" She nods so we start preparing.

It only takes a few minutes before we have a crudely made bed on the living room floor. Six blankets make up the padding, and we prop a bunch of pillows against the base of the couch. Lynn hands me a plate with a slice of cold pumpkin pie and then passes me a tub of whipped cream to dollop on top. The opening credits play while we eat our dessert. Before the first scene is over, my pie is gone. I turn and look at Lynn and put on my best puppy dog eyes.

*****

"Didn't you manage to eat an entire tub of whipped cream then?" Anne smiles fondly, and I nod vigorously. "Yeah! It was like three cups of cream! I still can't believe she let me do that. I'm pretty sure I was even dipping gummy worms in it at one point." I laugh at the screwed up look on Anne's face.

Reminiscing like this makes her pleasant to be around. It's not like she has an ulterior motive; she's just talking because she wants to. I wish my parents had done that.

"Do you remember that Halloween that you came for when you were younger?" I have to think for a moment.

"Like five years ago? Quinton was three, right? I remember."

"You remember the weird pictures we got –" I cut her off and exclaim, "Because of the cape!"

*****

"Hey, Alaina!" Anne is calling from downstairs. I sigh and set my book down. Tomorrow is Halloween, and I still don't have a costume, so I'm patching my sadness with a new book about wizards. I roll off the bed and jump down the stairs two at a time.

"What's up?" I speak to Anne's back. She spins around fast, flourishing a large black sheet. It shines in the light while she turns and I notice that it's been stitched by hand. "Surprise!" I stare at her, trying to figure out what the surprise is. She lays the sheet out on the table, and I realize it is a handmade cape. "You've been upset since we couldn't buy you a costume, so I made you one. Well, sort of. I made this cape, and I was wondering if you wanted to be a vampire or a witch. It could go either way." Anne looks at me, eyes wide "Is it okay?"

I smile and pick up the cloth. "Yeah, it's great, thank you." While I inspect the collar, I notice a small symbol on the corner. I can't tell what it's supposed to be. Anne looks as I run my thumb over the pattern. "That's a safety sigal. I'm not sure if I did it right, but I thought it could look spooky without being bad." I nod and smile again. "I think I'll be a vampire. Anne starts bustling around the house, throwing the rest of my costume together.

Shortly after, I look like a fresh recruit for the undead. My black cape wraps around my entire body, and it has a loop on each side for a finger to hold and open up like wings. Under my cape, I wear a tight blue shirt and skinny black pants. The outfit is completed with a pair of heavy combat boots, and Anne straightens my hair and helps with some vampire-esque makeup. I'm standing in front of the fridge, waiting for a picture so we can go trick or treating. Anne pulls Quinton to stand in front of me. "Pretend like you're biting the mummy!" I open up my wings and lean down, mouth open. There's a bright flash of light, and Anne yells out more pose directions.

*****

"I remember, the pictures where my cape was closed looked normal, but as soon as I opened the makeshift wings, the bottom half of my body disappeared, like a real vampire." A shiver runs down my spine, and Anne whispers, "I wonder if it was the symbol I sewed in."

I shrug, "I don't know, but it was creepy. Mom burned the cape last year."

Anne nearly swerves off the road from shock, and I grab onto the armrest to stay upright. "What! Why?"

I shrug. "Thought you cursed it. Weird stuff sometimes happens, like lightbulbs exploding when we talk about you.

I think that, along with the fact it was the only time you showed up for 4 years."

Anne falls silent, and I prop my elbow on the windowsill to peer outside. I can see a city in the distance. "Hey, is that where we're going?"

Anne peeks around my shoulder and nods, "Yup! That's Tepic, but first –" She points through the window on her side; we're heading up that way a bit to see San Sebastian. I think you'll like it; it's another historic district."

Less than twenty minutes later, we are pulling into a town that seems to be half the size of Colomo. All the buildings are whitewashed, the tiles of the road are arranged in arching patterns and appear to be freshly painted. The whole place seems to reflect the sunlight and look way brighter than the rest of the country. Anne points here and there, naming different buildings and offering history lessons. It takes us about fifteen minutes to creep through the tourist attraction at ten miles an hour. When we reach the side opposite where we entered, Anne parks on a cliffside and turns to me. "What do you think of this place?"

"Well, it's tiny. I can't believe anyone ever lived here." I reach over and roll the window down. "Plus, it's blistering hot! Why is everything so reflective?"

"They paint everything every year for the new batch of tourists, the society –" Anne's coming lesson is cut off by a bloodcurdling scream forcing its way through my throat. While she spoke, a large chicken flew through my window and is flying around the car.

Feathers fly and talons scratch while Anne tries to grab the bird. I can't stop screaming, I've never been afraid of chickens before, but I didn't know that they could be so vicious. A talon catches my arm and tears a hole in my flesh. Another talon nicks my nose. Finally, after many injuries being doled out, Anne pins the chicken's wings against its body and throws it from the window.

"Quick! Roll it up!" She yells loudly, but I can barely hear it. I feel like I've gone deaf from my own screaming. I reach down and start rolling the window handle, praying another one doesn't fly in.

Anne and I sigh at the same time and slump down. We sit in silence for a few minutes before both of us burst into laughter. Tears are rolling down my face. I can barely breathe from how hard I'm laughing. The whole situation is so ridiculous. Finally, after calming down, Anne sits up straight and pokes my shoulder. "Ready to go?"

I nod weakly. My body hurts now. *I didn't even know chickens could fly.*

*****

"Wow, this is amazing!" We are driving through a plaza in Tepic. Just ahead of us is a tall building with a glass top and a large gold statue standing guard. Parked nearby is an old-style red trolley. The sidewalks are made of a clean terracotta tile, and there's a huge water fountain in the middle of the square. Anne pulls the truck into an open parking spot, and we all climb out. I lift my leg and prop it on the edge of the truck bed to stretch while Anne surveys the area. "There's a taco truck over there. Do you guys want tacos or tamales for lunch?" I finish stretching my hamstrings and bounce on the balls of my feet. "Yes!" I can't help but exclaim from excitement. Tacos from trucks have become my favorite food, aside from gorditas at a little restaurant in Colomo. Anne laughs and retrieves her purse from behind the driver's seat. "Alright then, come on!"

I follow Anne, the kids walking between us, towards a large market on the other side of the square. Colorful stalls line the sidewalk, each holding something different to buy and accompanied by food trucks separating them. Bright yellows, blues, and reds pop at us from all sides, it's hard to decide where to start.

We walk up and down the path, browsing the pop-up shops. One only has cowboy hats, but each hat is painted with an intricate design. Another stall only has jewelry, but it all looks like traditional Latin designs, and everything is handmade.

After window shopping for a short time, we stop in front of a large blue truck. Parked sideways, we look up into a large window on the side and read the menu at the back of the kitchen on wheels. I settle on four pork tacos, Anne gets beef, and the kids each opt for a tamale.

Before long, we are lounging at one of the tables, eating. We take a long while munching on our lunch. It feels like a huge reward after our trip.

Once we finished eating, Anne takes us back to the truck and we drive through the rest of Tepic. There are tons of places to shop, huge city buildings; some historical, and others designed to look like modern offices. It takes us almost an hour to comb through the business district. Anne starts heading south afterward and pats my leg. "I want to show you the residential area," I nod and patiently wait while she drives.

"Ugh, what is that smell?" I wrinkle my nose up and try to take shallow breaths. The moment we enter the first neighborhood, a smell like rotten eggs descends on the car. Anne looks around as if she can see the waves of foul odors and she is searching for the source. "I think it must be the sewer system."

It takes everything in me not to retch and vomit out the window. I plug my nose and breath through my mouth as we drive past house after house. This would be a cute street if it weren't for the smell. Each residence is neatly lined up, with bushes accenting the front door. Every third house is painted a warm burgundy color, with a pale periwinkle home to the left and a tan stucco one to the right. "It's like someone used a cookie cutter to make these. They're all so perfect."

"Yeah, people do tend to call blocks like this 'cookie-cutter houses.' What do you think of them, though?"

We make it to the end of the road, and the horrible smell starts to clear. I wait to answer until I can breathe comfortably. "It's a cute neighborhood. If it weren't for the smell, it would be a nice place for anyone to live."

"Even us?"

"What do you mean? We have a house."

Anne sighs deeply and turns to latch the back window, closing Quinton and Mercedes off from our conversation. "I'm thinking about leaving Colomo. What if we come to move here, or to Guadalajara?"

I think for a moment before speaking carefully. "I think it could be good to leave. But I'm not sure how we would do here. You don't work, and I'm too young to." I do my best to maintain a calm demeanor, but inside, I'm freaking out. Numbers and scenarios start flying through my head. Anne currently owes the corner store owner over a thousand pesos. The two thousand that Anthony sends each week barely gets us through five days. Anne doesn't even have a job in

Colomo; how could she get a job here? Not to mention the fact that Mercedes and Quinton would need to be driven to school, we only have one car, and I'm too young to drive.

Anne sees the worry lines crease in my face and wraps her arm around my shoulders. "Don't stress honey, that's my job. It was just a suggestion. I would figure it out if we did come here."

I exhale slowly and nod. "Okay."

"Okay? We ready to head off now?"

I nod again. Anne reaches back and opens the back window, and we head out of the city the same way we came.

15

GUADALAJARA

"Mom! I'm cold!" Quinton's voice yelling through the window snaps me from my stupor. I sit up and realize the sun is setting. Anne slows the truck down and yells out the window, "We're almost there, just another ten minutes."

I hear a quiet "Okay" that gets snatched by the wind when Anne speeds back up.

"Are we almost there?" Anne nods, and I start bouncing in my seat. I'm excited to see another big city after Tepic. *I bet this one won't smell bad.*

I've spent a few hours in the car doing mental math, adding up numbers, and calculating potential income for if we move. I usually hate math class, but projects involving numbers and logic relax me. I stick a mental pin in my current scenario as we approach a large arch. The sign hanging from the middle reads 'Welcome to Guadalajara' Anne and I make eye contact, and our smiles creep in at the same time.

The sky is dark by the time we reach the middle of the city, but there are so many bright lights that it doesn't matter. This place almost reminds me of Las Vegas. Every building has at least one neon sign on its front. Bright streetlights break the sidewalk every few meters, leaving no patch untouched by an artificial glow. We pull under a bridge, and I notice neon lights are lining the underside. Anne parks next to the curb after we drive out from under the pass, and a large window set in a bubble-gum pink wall greets us. The front door has a neon pink sign on it, and the window is adorned with brightly colored stickers. I clamber out of my seat and onto the sidewalk. It's still warm from the sun that day, and I enjoy how it feels on my bare feet for a moment before slipping my sandals on.

Anne leads the way into the large store, the kids and I close on her heels. The door opens with a cold blast of air, and I can finally see what is inside – "Ice cream?" I feel giddy when Anne nods, I love ice cream, and we haven't had any since we left Oregon. "We're going to take a bathroom break and grab a treat before we stop for the night!"

I do a little happy dance and squeal. I probably look younger than the kids to the person manning the counter, but I don't care. I bolt to the bathroom and go as quickly as humanly possible.

Less than two minutes later, my eyes are glued to the frosted glass that separates me from tubs and tubs of creamy goodness. Rocky Road, Mint Chip, and Peanut Butter Swirl catch my eye, but then I notice some strange flavors I've never seen before. Horchata, Hibiscus, and Abuelitas. I'm not sure how those would taste, so I decide to stick to the classics.

After all of us are equipped with a large cup of ice cream, we pile back into the truck and take off down the road. As we drive, Anne explains that we will be staying with a friend. And she has a daughter around my age!

By the time we reach the friend's house, our treats are long gone. Anne parks in front of a long dark building and jumps out of the truck before any of us can follow. Confused, I roll down my window to ask if this is the place. It looks like no one is home, and cobwebs decorate the front, as if it's been left empty for years.

Before I can ask what's going on, Anne pulls back a heavy beaded curtain that I skimmed over earlier, and I see a light shining through the hidden alley. *Okay, creepy place it is.*

I follow Anne down a short hall that cuts through the empty building, and we emerge into a large courtyard. Music is playing loudly, yard lights shine, imitating the late evening sun. A tall woman in a bright green leopard print shirt runs and wraps Anne and me in a tight hug. Speaking rapid Spanish, it sounds like she is asking how the trip went. Anne chats with the woman for a minute before putting a hand on my shoulder and speaking in English, "Imelda, this is my daughter, Alaina." I bow my head awkwardly, not sure how to greet this stranger. The woman speaks to me in perfect English. "Hello, Alaina! It's so nice to finally meet you! I hope you enjoy staying with us."

I give Imelda a genuine smile and duck under Anne's arm to head back to the car for my bag.

*****

This family does not stop partying. Hours after we've arrived, their music is still cranked up to full volume, bright lights are still flooding every corner of the yard. Imelda showed us to a small cottage at the back; there was a room for me, each of the kids, and Anne. After getting settled in, we met the rest of the people here. Only half are Imelda's family. Her daughter, Yvonne, is a year older than me and it seems like she's allowed to do whatever she wants. Her little brother, who's name I don't remember, is Quinton's age, and they took off to play immediately. Mercedes made herself busy with the dog, and the rest of the family and friends' faces blended together until I couldn't tell or remember who was who.

"Hey, Lane!" I look up from my book and see Yvonne running across the courtyard. She stops in front of me, taking a deep breath; she leans down and puts both hands on my shoulders, and stares straight into my eyes. "Do-you-want-to-go-to-a-party?"

The way Yvonne pauses dramatically after every word makes me laugh "It's like ten o clock, shouldn't we be going to bed?" Yvonne shakes her head vigorously, shaking me with her. "No! It's fiesta time! Let's go!"

I sigh dramatically and stand up, "Alright, alright. Let's go" Yvonne takes my hand, and we walk out to the main road together.

Before long, we can see the brightly lit plaza. Even from twenty meters away, the bass of music vibrates the ground beneath us. The closer we get, the more excited. Yvonne and I chatter nonstop before we reach the square. It's brightly decorated, ribbons and flags hang everywhere, bits of confetti decorate the concrete pavers around a fountain spewing pink water.

When we start dancing, a group of girls our age, and boys that look older, surround us. We all dance for what feels like hours until a hand is pulling me from the hoard. Yvonne leads me away from the multitude of the crowd, and we sit on the edge of the fountain. She hands me a churro and a cup of funny tasting pink juice, which I take gratefully. I didn't realize how hungry dancing had made me.

"So, are you going to move here?" She speaks while chewing her churro, accidentally spewing sugar at the end of her question. I giggle and shrug, "I don't know; I might not mind it, though. This place is cool!" She nods fast, and I have to laugh again as more bits of sugar fly through the air.

We sit and talk for a long time, making it through a whole jug of pink juice, before standing together and walking back to her house. I nearly topple over after a few steps. *Who knew dancing could be so exhausting?* I turn around and snag one last look at the party. *This is the most fun I think I've ever had, unless you count smoking weed with Tyson in the woods.*

*****

A bright ray of sunlight is seeping through my eyelids; I crack them open and squint around. I'm in an unfamiliar room. Everything is white and lit up by the sun streaming through the window. I prop myself on my elbows while memories come flooding back. *We're at Imelda's.* I feel like I've been run over by a bus. My head is pounding, and it's like I'm moving through jello as I climb out of bed.

I hobble to the door, but before I can step through, Quinton zooms past on a scooter, knocking me back and causing a sharp pain to shoot through my skull. *What the hell?*

I wander around the courtyard before I spot the door of the main house. I see Anne, Imelda, her husband, and Yvonne leaning around the kitchen counter.

"What time is it?" I grit my teeth as I speak. The sound of my own voice hurts my head.

"Jeez, kiddo, you okay? It's almost noon, and you look like crap."

I nod slightly and breathe in before trying to talk. "I woke up with a migraine. I think I was up too late." Anne looks at me, concerned, but doesn't say anything else. I grab a piece of toast from the plate in front of her and wobble back to my room to nurse my headache. Before I'm out of earshot, I hear Yvonne tell Anne that I was hungover. *I don't have the energy to deal with that BS.*

*****

A light tapping sound wakes me from a dream about an octopus made of grapes. When I open my eyes, I see that the sun is low in the sky. *I must have slept for hours. What on earth is going on?* "Come in," I croak. The door squeaks open, and Anne walks in to hand me a cup of coffee.

"Good morning, sleepyhead. How are you feeling?" I pause and take a mental stock of my body. My thighs are sore, likely from dancing, and my headache is mostly gone, but my mouth is drier than the Sahara. "Better." I take a long gulp of the warm coffee and savor the relief it brings to my throat.

"Hm. So, Yvonne was saying that you got drunk last night…" She trails off, and I roll my eyes. "No way, I've never had alcohol. All I had to drink was some weird hibiscus juice she brought with our tacos." Then it dawns on me. *Oh my god. That was alcohol! She tricked me?*

Anne nods and starts moving my blankets, tucking me in. "Well, even if you didn't know it, welcome to the world of hangovers. Just stay in bed, drink that, and you should be fine in an hour." I nod, feeling grateful. For once, Anne is taking care of me, and it feels nice. I chug the rest of the warm liquid and snuggle into rest.

*****

Anne was right. An hour after coffee, I feel half human again. I stretch deeply after getting up and wander out of my room. The sun is starting to set, and the house is quiet. I poke my head into a couple of other rooms but don't see anyone, so I pull my shoes on and start walking down the road. It's strange, when we first arrived in Mexico, I felt the need to count my steps and keep a mental map no matter where I was. Now I'm not sure if I just don't care or if I feel comfortable here.

I make my way back to the plaza where I danced. It looks completely different now—no signs of confetti and loud music. But I swear you can see footprints worn into the concrete from the mass of people. The taco truck is next to the fountain, and Anne sits at one of the tables, back towards me. I walk up and tap her shoulder before sitting down. Anne smiles and pushes a plate of tacos towards me. "Where is everyone?" After asking, I take a huge bite, and the taste of freshly cooked pork makes my stomach rumble. I didn't realize how hungry I was.

"Imelda took the kids to some park. She said I should have a break. We figured you're old enough to handle yourself for a couple of hours," I nod and swallow. "Oh, sorry! I can go back to the house." Anne shakes her head, "No, kiddo, I'd rather hang out with you! We can walk around and see the sights a bit."

"Alright... Hey, how much longer are we staying here?" She looks at me with concern, and I sigh deeply before explaining. "I didn't know what I was drinking last night. Yvonne brought juice over and told me it was just that. I feel weird being here when someone got me drunk, and I had no idea."

Anne nods slowly, and we sit in silence while she thinks. "Well, we can go tomorrow morning. It's a bit late to make the drive now, and if we wait, we can stop for groceries on the way." *Okay, that works.*

We finish our meal quietly and walk around a few blocks together before heading back to Imelda's.

Part Three

16

SICK

Eck. I can't stop coughing, and my mouth is full of phlegm, which makes me want to throw up.

"Oh Alaina, what on earth is going on?" Anne flips on the bedroom light, and I catch a glimpse of my reflection in the mirror across the room. My face is pale and clammy looking, eyes watery, and my cheeks are hollow. I've been sick for a week, and it seems like I'm about to knock on death's door. *Who knew that four months in a new country would be all to make me kick the bucket?*

Anne places a hand on my forehead and worry forms in her brow. "I'm taking you to the clinic. I'll make you a cup of tea, and then we'll go."

I don't have the strength to do anything but nod once and collapse back into my pillow.

Sure enough, thirty minutes later, we are flying down the road. I'm wrapped in a thick blanket with no seatbelt because I couldn't get my arms to work correctly. We pull up to a small white building with two rooms, and Anne helps me inside. I slump into a plastic chair while Anne checks in with the receptionist.

Moments after their conversation ends, an older woman, probably Anne's age, beckons us into another room, with a typical hospital bed. The doctor helps me clamber up, and I wait while she reads her computer screen. "Do you have a history of pneumonia?"

I lift my head and look at her, my brain processing slowly. *Pneumonia…* No? I shake my head and try to speak. After a couple of croaks, I manage to whisper, "No, is that lungs?" My attempt at speaking sends me into a heavy coughing fit again, lungs rattling, phlegm filling the recesses of my mouth, the pain nearly topples me off the bed. *I want to die.*

The doctor puts her hand on my back in the middle of my fit, and when I finally compose myself, asks, *"Bronquitis?"*

"Bronchitis? Yeah, last year." I start coughing again, and the doctor nods and taps away at her keyboard. "I'm giving two prescriptions. One to help now, one will keep it away for two or so years."

Anne nods and thanks the doctor, and we head out of the office. I can't help but feel grateful. Anne is actually taking care of me. After helping me into the truck and climbing in herself, I slump onto her lap while she drives.

*****

The doctor was right. A week after taking the first pill, I'm almost back to normal. I've warmed up to Anne much more than before, and I'm actually starting to feel comfortable here. *Maybe I will be okay, living in Mexico. At least the medicine is good.*

17

KAREN

"Good Morning, Mom" I grab a bowl off the counter and flop into a chair, pouring myself a hefty serving of Trix. I don't remember when I started calling Anne 'Mom', but it finally wore on me after hearing it from the kids for so long. Anne stands and kisses my forehead before taking the rest of the dishes to the pila to wash them. "What do you want to do today?"

"Could we go to Vallarta?"

Anne stops scrubbing and thinks a moment, "Yeah, I'm sure we could! You'll have to let the kids know and find Mercedes some clothes," I nod and drop my spoon in my bowl. Before I can stand, Anne's phone starts ringing. I have to laugh; she has to be the only person in the modern world with one of the Nokia brick phones.

"Bueno?" She answers the phone, and I decide to eat a bit more cereal while she talks. "Oh, really? That's exciting! What time?"

"We'll see you then."

Anne clicks a button and sets the phone down. "Change of plans, kiddo, something exciting is happening!" I look up, waiting.

"My friend Karen is coming!"

"Uh… Karen, an American?"

"Mmm, she owns a house around the corner; she and her husband come every year. I think you'll like her."

All my previous plans to run flood back in. *Does this mean I could have someone to take me back to the States? But what's the point? Linda and dad don't want me.*

"Alright, sounds fun."

I finish off my breakfast, and we get ready to walk to Karen's.

*****

I don't know how I never noticed this house. It's enormous by Colomo standards. We are standing in front of the front gate looking in. She has to be the only person here that has a six-foot-tall fence around her property. The gate is on wheels and secured with a padlock. At the end of the driveway sits a large two-story house. It's covered in stucco-like every other place here, but somehow looks… Americanized. We make our way into the home and enter a huge kitchen, finished with tile floors, painted walls, and nice appliances. Next to it is an equally large dining room with a table long enough for fourteen people. Right of the dining room is a sitting area that takes up the rest of the downstairs.

"Anne! I'm so glad to see you" A short, plump woman with wild white hair waddles across the kitchen to hug Anne. She turns to me and puts both hands on my arms and squeezes. "You must be Alaina; I've heard so much about you! Welcome to La Casa de Roberts!" The woman laughs lightly and squeezes again before dropping her hands away. "My name is Karen, my husband is Phil, he's just upstairs."

I nod and try to smile politely. This woman has a weirdly bubbly personality for someone that chose to buy a house in a rundown impoverished town.

Karen guides us to the living room and points upstairs. "We added a few new rooms," I realize she's talking to Anne, and I tune out of the conversation. I daydream about the book I'm reading and wait to be spoken to.

*****

"Empanada?" I snap out of my thoughts and see a tray held in front of me. Tiny pastries that look like turnovers are lined up neatly in two rows. "Sure, thanks."

Karen beams at me as I take one of the treats. I bite into it, and the taste of warm caramelized apple fills my mouth. I look around and see that more people have shuffled into the house while I was zoning out. A few of the kids that run around town every day are here, eating off platters of baked goods displayed on the dining table. People pepper the various couches in the sitting room, and Anne is on the opposite end of the sofa from me. It seems the adults are having a lively conversation about Karen's adventures, but I can't be bothered to pay attention. I eat my mini apple pie in silence until Karen asks, "So, why did you decide to come here with your mom?" I freeze.

What? "Um..." I'm not sure what to say. I chew slowly and try to think. *Do I announce in front of everyone that I didn't want to? What if they try to get involved? Will I get sent back*

109

to the States where I don't have anyone anymore? Do I say I wanted to come?

After a very long pause, while the crowd waits for my answer, I just shrug. Anne laughs and covers, telling everyone a very doctored version of how we ended up here 134 days ago.

Soon enough, the conversation grows louder and strays from me. I pick up another empanada and hold onto it in case I'm faced with more uncomfortable questions.

*****

Hours after arriving at Karen's house, people finally start to disperse. *This lady is popular.* I shake my head. Over the short time we have been visiting, I watched Karen hand out at least 4,000 pesos, give away stuff from her collection of decorations, and present each child that walked in with a toy. I can't tell if she is genuinely a good person or if she is manipulative like Anne. *Maybe all of her stuff is stolen too.*

Finally, the last person leaves, and the house is empty except for our family. Our host sits on the couch opposite us, and looks at me intently, making me feel uncomfortable. "So, *did you want to come here?*" I look down and shuffle my feet. I don't know how to answer, I don't want to get in trouble, but I don't want to lie.

Anne nudges me and says, "It's okay." I sigh and look up, meeting Karen's gaze. "I didn't. I really loved my life before. But now that I'm here, my family doesn't care, so I'm happy to stay."

Karen nods while she thinks. "Well, I'm sorry about your family." She turns and gives Anne a strange look, almost like they both know something that I don't. "If you ever need anything, you let me know." Anne nods and reaches out to squeeze her friend's hand.

The whole exchange makes my stomach squirm. I feel like there is something I'm not being told.

*****

After two weeks of people rushing from all over Colomo to visit Karen, she announces she will be going back to the States early. Looking around town, you would think she announced God was dead. Forlorn faces are everywhere. Kids stop playing so loudly, and Karen is the only topic that locals care to talk about.

"Honestly, she kind of creeps me out. I'm glad she isn't sticking around for long." I take a long sip of coffee and peek at Anne over the edge of my cup, hoping that I didn't offend her. She laughs lightly. "I think it's because you don't know her. Karen and Phil have come here every year for the last forty-odd years. The town loves them"

"I just don't get it." I finish off my drink and head for my favorite reading spot. I pull out a book and pretend to read until I hear Anne humming while cleaning the kitchen. I reach into the back of my book and pull out a small crumpled notebook the size of my hand.

After a few months of being here, I started journaling, and while I'm happier than before, I still don't want anyone taking my journal - *like Linda used to*. Reaching into a fold of the hammock, I pull out a half-empty pen and let my thoughts flow onto paper.

18

CHRISTMAS IN COLOMO

We've been here for 161 days now. It's strange how much easier life has become. I'm getting used to living with siblings, and Anne has stepped up and been a "mom" for once. The only downside is that I can't go to school.

I stop writing and look around, realizing the house is quiet. I close the journal resting on my lap, swing my legs over the hammock, and step onto the cold cement floor. *I'll never get used to that.*

Once it's clear that the house is empty, I take my journal and stow it under my mattress where no one will find it.

I slide into a pair of slippers and pad into the kitchen for a snack. The entire counter is covered in wax paper, coated in peanut brittle and divinity. We're two weeks from Christmas, and it makes me feel a little sick to my stomach. I'm worried that Christmas won't be like usual. *Like Christmas at dad's house was ever amazing.* The truth is I hate holidays. Last year, dad and Linda asked what I wanted for Christmas. I said either a phone or an iPod. I just wanted to be able to listen to music like a normal kid, without lugging around a clunky CD player that was older than myself. I was so excited at the prospect. Christmas rolled around, and my cousins came over.

*****

"Oh my gosh, I heard that Chris got me an iPod for Christmas!" My two cousins and I are huddled in my room, whispering loudly. Kristin peeks around me before talking, "Where do you think he hid it? We should try to find it!"

I shake my head furiously. "No way, I don't want to risk not getting it, or worse. It's probably hidden in the laundry room anyway. That's where they hide everything." By 'they,' I mean my weird family unit, but my cousins are used to it by now. My mom and dad are married, but dad got sick years ago and told mom to find someone to do things with, so she met Chris. He's becoming a third parent. They try to hide it and make it seem like he's just a friend, but Chris has called mom his girlfriend in front of me before. Plus, friends don't take friends on expensive dates and buy them heaps of diamond jewelry. I don't really mind, though. Chris keeps mom calm, for the most part. When he's around, she doesn't hit me as much.

Marie stands abruptly and shakes me out of my thoughts. "Come on, let's go check out presents." I gawk at her. She is three years older than me, so I almost always do what she wants, but I've never scoped out gifts before opening them. After a lot of persuading, Kristin and Marie drag me downstairs, and we crouch by the tree. They do this every year. I anxiously look over my shoulder, but mom is nowhere to be seen.

Kristin picks up a gift with her name on it and gives it a light shake. "I think this is hair stuff" She sticks her tongue out in mock disgust, and Marie and I laugh. I start shuffling through the brightly wrapped packages, trying not to move any out of place, until I spot one near the back with my name. It's a small rectangular package, smaller than a red brick, but wrapped like one. I hold it up and wriggle my eyebrows at the girls. "It's the right size to be a phone" I laugh but then shake my head. "I bet it's not, though. It's heavy, but it's probably some decoration. My parents won't ever get me a phone". Marie smiles at me and hides a package she was holding. "Don't worry, if it's not, you can have my old one in a couple of months."

I smile wide. My cousins are always looking out for me.

*****

Five hours later, we are done with Christmas dinner, and the whole family sits around our huge living room. Grandma perches on the oversized couch with Auntie, Uncle Will, and Chris. Mom and dad sit on the small couch. My cousins, Zayne and Brody, are sitting on the floor near my brother, Jackson, and his girlfriend. Kristin and Marie sit next to me, furthest from the tree. Renee stands closest to the tree, passing out gifts until everyone has one with their name on it. On the count of three, we all tear into our wrapping paper. I get my parcel open and can't help but feel disappointed. It's another Game of Life. I've gotten this for Christmas three years in a row from different people. After everyone has opened their gift and said 'Thank you' to the giver, we go into another round of gifts. We continue like this for four rounds. My gift pile slowly stacks up. I was given a couple of books, a board game, and some art supplies. Nothing I'm upset over; I will definitely read the books and use the art stuff, but I want so badly for music. *Please, please, please. Even a cruddy MP3 player.*

The second to last round of gifts are handed out, and the heavy brick-like box is sitting in front of me. I carefully work my fingers under the paper, holding my breath while I unwrap. I breathe out heavily when I can finally see the front of the box.

NINTENDO 3DSi

Damn. It's hard to hide my disappointment. The DS is a great gift, and probably the only electronic I've ever been given that wasn't a hand me down, but I can't help but feel sad. I wanted something to listen to music on and a way to talk to my cousins. I look up and see Kristin jumping around. She drops to her knees next to me and holds out the box she just unwrapped, and I see a picture of a cell phone on the front. *Great.* Kristin is a year younger than me and always gets everything first. She had a DS when they first came out three years ago. *Now she gets a phone first. This isn't fair.*

*****

"Alaina! We're home" I leave my memories and look up from my snack to see Anne shuffling through the front door, weighed down with shopping bags. "What's all this?"

I help get all the bags onto the dining table, and Anne sighs dramatically. "Oh, you know, I just couldn't resist…. It's Christmas!" She does a funny dance in a circle. I laugh and peek into one of the bags. It is filled with red, green, and silver tinsel. Another bag has boxes of lights in it. *Maybe this Christmas won't be so bad.*

Anne dumps all the decorations out and starts sorting them into piles, explaining what she wants to do. Before long, all décor is in its designated room, waiting to be hung. As soon as I drop the last stack of light boxes, Anne grabs my hand and pulls me through the front door. "We're going to go get a tree now!"

I didn't know we could get Christmas trees in Mexico.

*****

An hour later, we are standing in front of Sam's club. Although it is a huge warehouse-style store, it sits in the middle of a strip mall. A 10-peso shop is on the left, and a restaurant on the right. Pine and Fir trees stand at attention out front, and a heavy wave of cinnamon assaults my nose when we step through the entry. "Whoa! Christmas is huge here!" I gawk at the shopping center. I never thought a store outside of America would be so heavily decorated. Tinsel drapes from the ceiling; wreaths are hung at every check-out register. A fully decorated tree guards the end caps of each aisle. The shelves look like an elf threw up red and green all over them. I laugh at how ludicrous everything looks. *This store is like Costco on crack.* We spend over an hour walking up and down the aisles before Anne stops. She hands me two hundred-peso bills and whispers, "Okay, I want you to do stockings this year. I'll do yours, but you do Mercedes and Quintons." I nod and pocket the cash.

I better run quickly before I lose the chance.

I glance at the kids and hope they don't see me leave. They'll probably both cry and try to chase me down.

I take off and head for the front door, weaving through people, walking as fast as possible without drawing attention to myself. I don't know how people here feel about children on their own. I pass a giant stack of books near the last check-out stand. *Maybe I should grab a book for myself?* I shake my head and focus on my current mission. *I must get out of here, quickly.* I dodge people walking through the entrance and try to walk casually down the sidewalk. I don't know why, but I feel like I just got away with something huge. I don't want a clerk to stop me.

I take a sharp right turn when I make it past the trees and walk briskly, looking over my shoulder to make sure I wasn't followed. *Why am I so anxious?* I know why. This is the first time I've had money in hand since getting to Mexico and the first time I've been able to leave Anne's side.

After a short walk, I stop and look up. The ten-peso store sign is glowing brightly, even though it is the middle of the day. I take a deep breath and walk in, mentally drafting a shopping list. After twenty minutes, I walk back out of the small Mexican dollar store, loaded with bags. Anne is in for a big surprise and she has no idea. I grin and make my way towards the Sam's club entrance.

*****

"Hey Alaina, flip that switch, will you?" I reach behind Anne, who is crouched next to our stubby Christmas tree, and flick a light switch up. Brightly colored lights come to life, woven between the tree's droopy branches. I giggle when I look down. The bottom half of the tree remains dark. For some reason, the box of lights Anne bought are half faulty, and now she is trying to fix them. "I'm telling you, there is just one light bulb that, once it's replaced, will bring the whole thing back to life!" Anne is insistent, but I don't quite believe her.

I turn the light back off and crouch down next to her and look at the wires. It only takes me a few seconds to spot an exposed area of one of the cords. "There! We need to patch that," I point before jumping up and running to grab a roll of tape. Anne stands and waits next to the light switch while running back to the room and starting taping. "So, I was thinking, I may message dad to say Merry Christmas." Anne makes a disgruntled sound, so I stop talking and finish patching the wires.

"Okay, almost done. When I wrap this last bit, I'll flip the switch-" a flash of blue light cuts me off.

117

Bright cobalt bleeds into my vision, and it's all I can see for what feels like twelve minutes. The room disappears, and electricity tingles on my arms. My brain goes numb. A buzzing fills my ears. I blink rapidly to clear the blue. At least, I think I'm blinking. I can't feel what my body is doing.

Finally, the fuzzy silhouettes of Anne, Mercedes, and Quinton come back into view. The blue pulses and fades slowly until I can see the green of the tree and grey of the walls again. Although, I was standing right next to the tree before, now it is four feet away.

"You okay, kiddo?" It takes a moment to focus on Anne's face. "Um, I think so?" My tongue feels heavy and numb. "How long was I out?"

"Only a few seconds." *Really? It felt like ages.* "What happened?" I walk to a chair in the corner and sit down. My legs feel like jello, and I don't trust myself to stand. Anne comes over and squats in front of me. "Well, I'm not sure. I heard 'flip the switch,' so I did, and you sorta stood and took a few steps backward." I shake my head, trying to clear the residual buzzing feelings.

"I think you electrocuted me." I try to stay calm, but I can't help but wonder. *Did she do that on purpose?*

*****

"Jingle bells, Batman smells!" I'm yelling in a sing-song tone, teaching Quinton the version of Jingle Bells that was taught to me at his age. Mercedes laughs so hard she almost falls off her chair.

After fixing up the lights, Anne decided to run and grab dinner to go. It was the perfect time for my secret project – gifts for Anne. We've just finished wrapping everything, and

I thought this would be a good pass time until she came home. Quinton gets excited and runs towards me, matching my pitch, "Robin laid an egg!" Before I know it, his hands are on my stomach, pushing me backward. I topple over, and my head hits the concrete wall behind me. Loud, ringing echoes through my ears and the room goes fuzzy for the second time. After being electrocuted less than two hours earlier, I don't understand why he would hurt me.

Anger burns through my chest, and I stand as quickly as I was pushed over. My brain disconnects, and without thinking, my arm swings forward.

It's like I'm watching my body move in slow motion. My hand connects with Quintons back as he turns away from me. A loud clap booms as skin connects with skin.

"ALAINA!" Anne's yell from the front door, combined with Quintons yelp of pain, brings me back to real-time, and my thoughts finally catch up with what just happened.

My hands fly to my mouth, and a bright red handprint on Quintons back glares at me. *I've never hit anyone. Why did I do that?*

Anne rushes over to tend to Quinton's injury while I babble, trying to explain what happened. "He pushed me, and hit my head, and – " The look on Anne's face makes me snap my mouth shut. I turn and walk into the bedroom, head down. *I am going to get my ass beat.*

*****

Just under an hour later, Anne opens the curtain and pokes her head in, causing me to flinch. "Quinton is okay. Do you want to talk about that?" Tears form in my eyes, and I can't make myself speak. I expected to be hit by her. I've never

119

been asked to talk about what caused my behavior. I shake my head, and Anne walks over to sit next to me. Draping her arm around me, I cower inward, terrified she is going to hurt me. Years of physical punishment have changed my expectations of others.

Instead, Anne hugs me tightly and whispers, "It's okay, feelings are hard." A croaking sound escapes my throat before sobs rack my body. I shake and cry while Anne holds me, as a mother should.

19

BELLE

"Hey, you want to see something new?" I look up from my book and peer at Anne across the table.

"I don't know, we see something new every week. What else could there be?"

A wide grin takes over Anne's face, and her eyes sparkle. I notice that when she smiles, she looks young, like the 42 odd years she actually is. When her smile fades, age etches its way into the wrinkles around her eyes and mouth, and her cheeks sag. A life of stress and running from everything has aged her by at least 15 years.

I slide my bookmark into place and stand, heading to grab shoes and a purse to put my book and DS in.

*****

One short drive later, we enter a small town, although bigger than El Colomo. Anne calls this place Bucerias and tells me about how it is her favorite place. There's a small shop that makes amazing Horchata con Nuez and ice cream. As we pass the town's plaza, I glance down an alley between two buildings and do a double-take. Lining the beach are giant sand sculptures; castles, mermaids, sea creatures, and more.

Anne parks the truck, and we walk down the grit-covered path to see the art. Many pieces stand taller than me and look like they've had days spent on them.

We approach the mermaid, and I study the sculpted figure. Her fins appear to float just above the sand as if she was in mid-kick when she was caught. Each scale on her tail has small swirling patterns carved in. Her skin has small patches of scales, with tiny scars elsewhere. I touch the mermaid's hard stomach gently. The sand has no give, as if once it was pushed into place, it became bone.

When my eyes reach her face, I'm taken aback. It looks as though I'm peering into the sea. The artist glazed the sand of her eyes to reflect the ocean behind us. Her hair is the only thing left unfinished. Stray strands frame her face, but the rest of her long curls are unsculpted, lying in a wet lump next to her.

Anne takes my hand and pulls me out of the trance this beautiful piece of art has me trapped in. I can't speak, I'm blown away by the fact that someone could turn sand into marble.

Anne explains that there is a sculpting contest every year in January. "Judging will take place in a couple of days. I think on the 10th."

I vow that next year, I will participate. My sketches are always realistic. Now I want to turn sand into stone too.

We make our way through the town, wandering past stalls of various things for sale, stopping into the horchata shop, and grabbing two large cups of cinnamon filled drinks to go. After a couple of hours of exploring, we stop at the local internet café. I pick a computer while Anne pays for an hour of internet access. As soon as the old box with a fuzzy screen lights up. I log in to check Facebook, and I'm shocked to see a notification.

'LINDA DAVIS: Dear Alaina...'

Message received December 18th, 2011

I grab Anne's arm and point, and her face looks grim. "Well, you better open it."

I click on the blue icon and hold my breath while scanning the first message I've received in months.

*****

18 Dec 2011, 01:18

"Dear Alaina,

Since I can't sleep, it seemed like a good time to wish you a Merry Christmas. We all miss you very much during the holidays. Hopefully, you are doing well, and you are okay. I know you told dad not to worry, but it's hard not to. We worry every day.

I will update you on everyone. Aunt Malley's family is fine, and Kristin misses you a lot. Renee's family is good too, and Elise is walking now and really cute. Jacob and Casey are growing fast, and Casey talks up a storm!

We have a new home on ¾ acre of land, and it's in the city, so we are close to everything, but it's better for dad because it seems like we are out in the country. It's private, and there are huge trees around the property. We have a chicken coop and are getting four chickens soon (that is the limit in the city). I just finished writing a 40-page paper and presenting it. That was my Senior Capstone. I have four classes left: two

123

in January and two in March. Graduation is in June. Time goes by fast.

I love you very much, and I know that you know that. Please write me back if you are allowed to and let me know how you are doing.

Love, Mom"

* * * * *

04 Jan 2012, 11:35

"Dear Alaina,

I just wanted to write and let you know that I put Belle to sleep this afternoon. She has been a good dog all these years, but for the last year has had a bad heart problem, and her medicine just wasn't working to correct it any longer. She was also deaf and could not see well. The last couple of weeks, she was really tired and coughed all the time, so I needed to do this. It's been a tough day.

Love, Mom"

* * * * *

"It sounds like life is pretty normal over there." I feel numb as I give Anne the rundown of news I received. *I don't know how to feel. Was it worse when I got no messages? Or worse that everyone seems fine. How was there a message in December that I missed? I logged on before Christmas.*

I close out of the messenger window and take a deep breath. I don't know what to write back.

20

ANTHONY

"Okay, great. I'll see you soon then. I love you." I look up from my DS while Anne finishes her phone conversation and eye her through the doorway suspiciously. *Who is she talking to? Please be Lynn coming for a visit.*

Anne walks into the room and beams at me, "Anthony will be here tomorrow!"

CRASH! My game system clatters to the ground before I can stop myself from dropping it. Quinton and Mercedes run into the room at the same time, yelling excitedly. *No. It can't be.*

After 207 days in Mexico, Anthony is finally coming down. I'm terrified. I may have grown to like Anne, but I can't ever like or tolerate living with him.

Of course, Anne doesn't know this. My brain pulls Anne's memory forward, suggesting moving, and I spring up from my swinging seat. "Wait, I thought you were thinking about leaving before he got here?"

Anne purses her lips and looks at the kids pointedly.

I wasn't supposed to say anything around them, so I try to recover. "I mean to plan a surprise." I fill my tone with fake happiness, but inside I am trembling with fear.

*****

"Anthony!" Anne squeals like a little girl as the front door opens. A man with very dark, wrinkled skin steps through. With broad shoulders and average height, his frame appears to be worn with age, but large muscles from years of farm work ripple through his arms and make him look younger.

I cower inward as he approaches the dining table. His dark eyes catch mine, and he winks, which makes me feel sick to my stomach. Anne wraps her arms tightly around Anthony, and the kids run in to jump on him.

Who knew a sixty-three-year-old man could support the weight of two kids and an obese woman?

I shovel the last bite of my lunch into my mouth and duck around the happy family to drop my plate in the pila, before slipping silently out the door. *There's no way I'm staying here with him. It's time to plan.*

*****

Less than an hour later, I set my stick down and review my checklist written in the dirt. After a quick read through, I nod to myself and pick up a wispy tree branch, running it over the markings and making the dry dirt blend together. It takes just a few moments for the remnants of my planning to disappear.

Time for step one; find out how much a bus ticket costs.

I start walking away from the wide river that separates El Colomo from the forest, and head towards the bus station.

A few minutes down the road, the rumble of exhaust makes me look up, and I see Anne's green truck barreling down the road towards me. Anthony sits behind the driver's seat, and Anne fills the passenger. Both kids are standing in the back, hands in the air as if they are rooted in place and can't possibly fly out.

I jump out of the way, and Anthony slows to a stop in front of me. Anne pokes her head through the cab and motions at the truck bed, "Get in, kiddo, we're going to the swimming holes."

I try to protest, but the kids hop down and start pushing me towards the back.

A short drive later, Anthony parks in front of a sizeable rock-filled basin; a tall cliff stands guard behind it. Anne leads the way across the lower swimming hole's remnants, and we start climbing up a steep dirt path hidden in the trees. A loud rumbling echoes through the trees, and as we climb, it grows louder.

After fifteen minutes, we emerge through an arch of tamarind branches, and I see a crystal pool reflecting the low hanging clouds. The second swimming hold is larger than a pond but smaller than a lake. The surface of the water in front of us is completely still, like glass protecting the fish inside. A waterfall breaks the surface on one end of the pool, cascading down from another tall cliff, while a small stream trickles from the opposite side, down towards the first basin we parked in front of.

Anthony steps forward, pushing Anne and myself out of the way, and looks around slowly before taking a running start. He leaps from a rock that protrudes out over the water and breaks the picturesque pond with a loud splash. Quinton and Mercedes follow close on his heels, both yelling as they fly through the air, and I have to laugh.

Before long, I find myself perched on a rock inside the swimming hole. Anne, Anthony, and the kids paddle and kick all over, but I'm terrified to leave my spot.

"Come on, kiddo! Come swim!" Anne calls from a few meters away. I shake my head vigorously. "Can't, sorry!" I never fully learned how to swim, and the depth of the pool scares me. The water is so clear that I can't tell if I could touch the bottom or if I'll get sucked down too far to breathe.

Anne makes her way over and joins me to air dry. "So, where exactly are we? I didn't know this was here."

Anne starts explaining. There are three swimming holes, the locals have a name for it, but she can't remember. The bare, bottom one usually is full by this time of year, but there wasn't enough snow on the mountain this time.

This is the second pool we are in, and the third is a long rock climb straight upwards. "Could we go up there?" Anne shakes her head. "Not unless you want to see some cougars." Anne starts pointing around to various spots hidden in the trees and telling me about what animals lurk beyond.

A shiver runs down my spine. I can't tell if it's a breeze that passed or that we are less than ten meters from a cougar's den.

I really can't wait to ditch now.

*****

By the time we finish swimming and start towards the truck, the sun is dipping below the horizon. *I won't be able to visit the buses today. My plan will have to wait until tomorrow.*

I comfort myself with the fact that I know Anthony has at least two thousand pesos in his wallet that I can take after I know how I'll be leaving.

After we reach the house, I collapse onto the bed. Moments after closing my eyes, I fall into an abyss of nightmares.

21

HORRIBLE CHILD

I feel something move on my leg, causing me to come to from my deep sleep. I lie still for a moment, mind fuzzy, trying to figure out if I felt it in a dream or if there is something in bed with me. I feel the light pressure from a hand on my thigh again and freeze. Not something.

Someone.

I stay still and mentally take stock of my surroundings. Quinton is snoring lightly across the room, and Mercedes is curled in a warm ball to my right. The edge of the bed is weighed down by someone sitting there.

No. Please don't.

I open my eyes when the fingers trail a few centimeters upwards, and I see Anthony's silhouette just inches from where I'm laying. I take a sharp breath in and almost scream when I see him raise a finger to his lips. His hand grips my upper thigh, and dread creeps in. I hazard a look down and see he isn't wearing any pants.

I reach down and try to move his hand away, and he makes a *tsking* sound and tightens his grip.

While I try to think my way out of this, I realize he is sitting at a weird angle, like he's stretching to reach over me. *That's not right...*

Oh. Oh no.

I turn my head to the right and catch a glimpse of his hand working to pull the cover off of Mercedes' tiny body, which is wrapped tightly in the heavy quilt.

No. No. This is not happening again. Doing it to me was one thing. I'm done.

I sit up quickly and push Anthony backward, tearing his hands off myself and my little sister, forcing him to stand. Whipping off my blankets, hot rage spreads through every inch of me. Before I can process my own thoughts, I feel flesh connect with bone. My eyes and brain focus, and I realize I've formed a fist with my right hand, and it is now crushing his beaked nose.

Anthony's yell pierces through my sleepy fog and wakes everyone else up. Suddenly, lights are flipped on through the house. Anne runs and stares in shock while the two kids sit up, still half asleep.

"She is a horrible child! She won't stay!" Anthony is yelling at the top of his lungs. I'm too shocked to move. *I can't believe I hit him. Holy shi-*

"Alaina! What are you thinking!" Anne's shrill voice brings my focus back, and I stare at her blankly. She repeats the questions again, somehow in a higher tone than before.

My mind starts moving at hyper speed. *What did I do? I can't tell her what he was doing to me. Last time, she nearly beat me to death. She won't believe me if I tell her what I saw. I*

131

look Anthony up and down and realize his nudity must have been a trick of the moonlight. He is wearing a near skin-tight tank top and briefs. *She definitely won't believe me since he's clothed. Well, I guess if I get hit, I get hit.* "He was touching me and Mercedes." I stand firmly in place and try to keep my voice strong without raising it.

Anne blanches and turns to Anthony, a questioning look taking over her features. Anthony is almost yelling when he speaks, "No! I came to check on my girls. I was tucking them in!"

I've never hated hearing his deep, accented voice more than in this moment. *How can he lie so easily?* I brace myself, waiting for a blow.

It doesn't come.

Anne looks around at all of us before sighing, "we'll figure this out in the morning. You" she snaps and points at Anthony. "Back to bed, stay out of the kid's room."

She gives me a reproachful look before turning on her heel and walking out, Anthony close behind.

I reach up and close the curtain that makes up our bedroom door and sit on the edge of the bed.

Breathe. Inhale. Exhale. It will be okay. I mentally coach myself through breathing for a few moments before lying back down. This is the first time I've ever stood up to him directly. It feels... *Weird.*

22

SHE RAN AWAY

A ray of sun shining directly onto my face wakes me early in the morning. I prop up on my elbows, rubbing sleep from my eyes, and trying to come to. The previous night's memories flash through my mind, and I feel sick to my stomach. *I wonder if he was serious about kicking me out.*

One way to find out.

I swing my legs over the edge of my bed and stretch deeply before trudging through the house and into the kitchen. It's oddly quiet. I peek into Anne's room and see that it's empty. Both kids are still asleep, but both adults just left us.

I pour myself a large bowl of fruit loops and perch on the kitchen counter. Halfway through my very slow breakfast, I hear footsteps outside. The front door swings wide open at the same moment that my feet hit the floor. Anne walks in, arms full of bags and hand gripping a stack of papers.

"Uh... Morning. What're you doing?" Anne sets the bags down and heads to sit at the dining table without saying anything. I follow and sit next to her while she lays out the crumpled documents.

The top of one page reads 'PUERTO V TO TIJUANA'

I look at Anne, puzzled. She breathes in deeply before speaking. "Anthony was serious about you not staying. I told him that he isn't going to get rid of my daughter, so he told us all to go." My heart drops into my stomach. When I finally get to the point of accepting this life, we have to leave it behind. "So, what's the plan?"

Anne points at the tickets in order as she speaks, "So, we'll take a bus from Vallarta up to Tijuana, then a Greyhound from there to Monmouth." I jump in my seat. "Monmouth? Does that mean I'm going back to...?" I trail off. I'm not sure what to call it anymore.

Anne shakes her head. "No, of course not; you remember Karen? Well, she and her husband live on the outskirts. They'll have us stay with them until we can figure life out. They have a ton of spare rooms, and we can get you enrolled in school." My stomach flips. *School! I've missed school so much in the last eight months.*

"When do we go?" I can hardly contain my excitement, and I bounce in my seat a bit. Anne still looks less than pleased. I steady myself and take a good look at her face. She seems tired. The wrinkles around her eyes are deeper than usual, and her cheeks look thinner than normal. Somehow, I don't think she wanted to agree to Anthony's terms.

My heart softens towards her a bit. *She chose me over him.*

I get lost in my thoughts before I notice Anne is pointing at the corner of one of the papers. I lean over to read, February 2nd, 2012. *That's next week! We have our work cut out for us.*

*****

Six days after the Anthony debacle, we have yet to see or hear from him. It seems that Anne has come to terms with the situation and is happy to be planning a trip again. Mercedes, Quinton, Anne, and I sit around the dining table. Anne has a list and all our passports and birth certificates out. "Alright, so I will be keeping all of this in a fanny pack. You three are responsible for your bags." She looks at the kids, "You two, keep your pack of clothes on your back or by your feet at all times." She looks at me, then smiles, "You should be fine; you're old enough to keep track of yourself. I'll have the big suitcase and backpack with the rest of our stuff.

Anne stands and looks around the house, pausing and looking pensive, before clapping loudly, "Let's go, everyone!"

$$*****$$

This road trip feels like it's moving much faster than the trip down into Mexico. Before I know it, we are nearing Tijuana. The bus has stopped a few times for fuel, at which point we all swarm into a rest stop for bathroom breaks and snacks. Each stop only lasts about twenty minutes, then nearly fifty people pile back into the silver bullet looking vehicle, and we are back on the road.

Ten minutes outside of the city, Anne motions me to lean in. "So, this might be a little difficult to get back. Normally there's a problem with my passport. And, since we are walking across instead of driving, things can get a little hairy. Whatever you do, I need you to stick with the kids." I nod and sit back in my seat; my heart is thumping loudly. I'm not sure why, but I feel scared to go back to the US. *What if things have changed?*

135

The bus slows to a stop in front of a large white building with blue windows. The driver's voice crackles over the loudspeaker, but people are already moving and drawing the static out. Anne nudges me, and I stand, pulling my duffle bag over my head before picking up Mercedes' backpack and securing it over my shoulder. Both kids grin up at me and take each of my hands. Quinton pats my arm "Don't worry, we'll help you."

A smile forms on my lips, and I'm less scared than before. *Who knew an eight-year-old could settle my nerves so easily?*

We exit the bus in single file and regroup in front of the wide building. It reminds me of a cross between a courthouse and an airport. The windows are shockingly blue, and the white bricks of the structure shine brightly in the mid-afternoon sun. Anne starts off in front of me, Mercedes by her side, and Quinton and I follow close behind. The door opens with a whoosh, a blast of cold air washes over us. A few steps in and the floor is moving beneath us, carrying a crowd of people down a long hallway.

We step off the human conveyor belt and into a large white room. Scanning around, I see counters lined up in front of us, with turnstiles separating them. To the right is a large chamber that someone is walking through, also tinted blue. A man is being detained outside of the chamber, and I see the officer next to him inspecting an apple. The contrasting red color of the fruit looks out of place.

We walk towards one of the counters where a young woman sits. She is dressed in a light blue uniform, blending perfectly with the other border patrol officers and the building itself. She waves Anne through, who scans her passport, then walks through the turnstile. Quinton is next, then Mercedes. Finally, I step up, set my passport face down on the scanner plate, and wait for the loud Beep to tell the woman I can move forward.

The approval doesn't happen. Instead, the officer gets a puzzled look on her face. She speaks into her radio, words muffled by her hand. Anne looks anxious while we wait, bouncing back and forth on each of her heels. A tall thin man approaches, short spiky hair glinting under the light. *Someone loaded up on gel today.* He takes my passport and motions for me and Anne to follow him to his desk.

"So, your passport has a yellow flag on it. Any idea why?" Before I can answer, Anne, steps forward, "Yes, sir, I'm sorry, Alaina ran away when she was younger. The flag must not have been removed. It's been years since we tried to travel internationally."

His brow furrows as he reads his screen. Time stops moving. For one long minute, my breathing echoes in my ears. Anne's nervous bounce slows. I turn and look at the officer with the apple and watch as it arcs in slow motion, heading for the bottom of a trash bin.

Finally, he speaks, and time returns to normal "Okay, I'll just put a note in here. Go ahead and move to the scanner." He gives me a reassuring smile and holds out my passport.

I exhale slowly. *We made it?* We move quickly through the long blue chamber. In the end, the apple guy asks us a list of questions, ending with "Do you have anything to declare?" My heart stops for the second time today.

I was taken out of the country illegally, and now we're coming back illegally?

Anne shakes her head answers for all of us, "We have a couple of granola bars in that backpack, but nothing that's not commercially packaged"

Oh, he meant food.

He waves us through, and we step through yet another blue door into the bright sun of California.

23

THE ROBERTS RESIDENCE

One very long ride later, we are standing at a bus stop in the dark. The sun has long since set, and clouds block out the stars. We sit in silence to wait for Karen to pick us up. Mercedes and Quinton are slumped together on the bench, fast asleep, and I consider joining them until a white SUV pulls up next to us.

A plump woman steps out. Standing a full head shorter than Anne, they look like a comical pair when Karen wraps Anne in a hug. "How was the trip? I bet you're all exhausted."

Anne nods and motions at the young kids behind us. "Yeah, some of us barely made it." The two friends erupt into laughter as if that was the funniest thing either of them had ever heard.

We all pile into Karen's car. The kids doze off immediately after being buckled in, and I feel my eyelids start to droop as we drive away.

*****

Twenty-five minutes later, a large bump startles me awake. Karen is driving up a long winding driveway. I peek through the window and see a large log cabin style house built into the side of a hill. The yellow toned lights shining through the front windows give off a welcoming feel, and the log patterns on the outside of the structure strike a feeling of sturdiness in me.

Once safely parked in front of the large garage, we pile out of the car, forgetting our bags for the night. A quick tour through the house ends in a bedroom on the third floor. The room is large and a similar shape to a circus animal cracker box. The bed in the middle of the room has a makeshift headboard made from a shelf packed tightly with books. A handmade quilt spread at the foot promises a good night's sleep. Karen steps through the door and smiles at me. "This will be your room!" I drop myself on the edge of the bed and look up at her. "For how long?"

I see a shadow of sadness pass through the old woman's eyes before she answers, "As long as you and your Mom are here, honey."

She turns and leaves the room, letting me give in to my exhaustion.

*****

"Good morning, sunshine!" Anne calls out as I hop down the last step. I look up and grin at the picture in front of me. Karen, Phil, Anne, Quinton, and Mercedes sit around a long antique dining table. The table itself is piled high with platters of eggs, bacon, sausage, biscuits, and fruit. I drop into the open seat and start serving my plate. We've been at Karen's house for nearly two weeks now, and I'm still not used to the amazing breakfasts I wake up to daily. I've become comfortable in this new routine.

Before I can start eating, Anne sets a pile of papers in front of me. "What's this?" I lean over and read the title - CENTRAL HIGH SCHOOL REGISTRATION

I nearly choke on a grape and look at Anne. "You mean I'm going to school?" Anne nods and smiles widely, "The last term of your freshman year starts in a week. What do you think?"

"Yes! Yes! I can't wait!" I almost start crying, overwhelmed with excitement.

I shovel my food down quickly and start running around the house, looking for a notebook and pen. *I have to make a list of supplies and get ready. I need to choose my classes. Oh my gosh, I can't believe this is happening!*

An hour later, I've finished filling in the registration packet, and my list is complete. Anne walks up behind me and squeezes my shoulder. "Hey, come on downstairs; we need to do a couple of things before I can turn that in."

*****

Perched on a wooden stool, I watch as Anne types 'I ran away' in the search bar and scrolls through webpage after webpage. She finds what she's looking for and scribbles a phone number into a notepad, followed by a couple of sentences.

"Alright, so here's the deal, kiddo. To get your school records without alerting the police, you need to call this number and say you've run away." I stay quiet while I try to process what she's saying.

"So, I have to lie? If I lie, I get to go to school?"

141

Anne pats my leg. "It's not really lying. Your dad doesn't want you back. But yes, after this, we can get you enrolled in school."

I nod and take the phone she's holding out. I press the numbers slowly, nerves making my hands shake. The line rings once. Twice. *CLICK*. "Hello, National Runaway Hotline, this is Amy. How can I help you?" The voice, on the other end, sounds sweet and comforting. I take a deep breath and read out the prompt Anne wrote down for me "Hello, my name is Alaina Franklin, I ran away last year, and now I need to get the missing case closed so I can go to school."

I hear a keyboard clacking on the other end before the woman speaks again, "Okay, Alaina, can you tell me where you are right now?" I look up and see Anne shaking her head. "Um... No. I want to be able to get my school records so that I can get into High School. Can you help?"

A pause follows my question. "Sure, sweetie. I do need to ask some questions first."

"Okay."

"First up, why did you run away?" Anne is scribbling furiously as Amy talks. I glance down at the notebook before answering. "Um, my parents abuse me, so I left"

Another pause. I hear a click before Amy asks another question. "Can I ask what school you want to enroll in?" Anne shakes her head again, and I tell Amy no.

The line delays again before the woman's voice crackles through. "Alright Alaina, why don't you give me your phone number, I'll see what I can do to help and call back in a couple of days."

I read off another phone number written in front of me, and Amy and I say goodbye. The line clicks twice and goes dead.

Anne closes the notebook and smiles at me. "Good job, kiddo! Now we wait, and you'll be back in school in no time!"

I nod and smile back, weakly. I don't feel right about that call.

24

1-800-RUNAWAY

I stare into my bowl of soup, thoughts wandering around me. Anne prods my arm and snaps me out of my daze. "Hey, what're you thinking?"

I sigh deeply. "Well, I was hoping we could get registered for school this week, but it's been three days since that woman said she'd call back."

"Well, let's call her then!" Anne hops up from her seat and motions for me to follow her downstairs. "Can we do that?" I call after her but receive no answer, so I trot downstairs and follow her into the office.

Within moments Anne has the phone and notebook in hand and is dialing the number. She hands me the phone while it rings and scribbles down more notes. "Hello, National Runaway Hotline, this is Ethan. How can I help you?" This time, a man's voice filled with static comes through. I stutter out my introduction and explain that I called a few days prior and spoke to Amy. Ethan starts clicking keys. "Okay, here we go. I found your file, Alaina. Give me one moment to read it." There is a long pause while I wait. The line clicks, and the static clears halfway through. After what feels like five minutes, Ethan speaks again. "Alright, Alaina, it looks like Amy put even more notes in here than I thought. Do you mind telling me what you were after, in your own words?"

I read Anne's notes before speaking, "Sure, so, I ran away last year. Now, I want to go to school, but I can't get my school records until the missing person case is dropped." There is another click that echoes through the speaker. "Um, what's that sound?"

"I'm not sure what sound you mean."

"I hear clicking..."

"Our phone system can be a little funny sometimes; maybe it's that."

"Oh, okay. Anyway, do you think you can help? Amy said she would call back and never did."

"Well, Alaina, it seems Amy did try, but the phone number she was given wasn't valid; it connected to a google voicemail account, like a burner phone. Do you know what that is?"

I tell him no, and we chat for a few more minutes. By the end of the call, Ethan assures me that he'll be able to help, especially since we got to talk for so long. It gave him heaps of information for the case. I'm not sure what he means, but I feel better now. When I go to hang up, the line clicks twice before going dead. I try to shake it from my mind, but it's so strange.

Anne tucks the phone and notebook away and pulls up a website. The URL reads 'www.ABCleaning.com.' "Well, do you want to help me with this until bed?"

I nod and scoot in close to the computer, and we start working on an ad for the company that Anne wants to start. We work for hours before a loud BANG behind us stops our conversation.

25

THE DETECTIVE

A deep voice booms behind me. "Freeze! Anne Franklin, you're under arrest for first-degree custodial interference, kidnapping in the third degree, theft on 14 counts in the first degree –"

What's going on? My brain starts to go fuzzy, and the booming voice fades away. It feels like the world is moving in slow motion. I turn my chair around to see the room behind us, full of people in blue uniforms. My eyes find the voice source, a tall man with sandy blonde hair and blue eyes stands just a few feet behind Anne. One hand is holding a pair of handcuffs; the other is resting on a holster on his hip. My eyes widen as Anne stands up from her chair and disappears into the sea of blue. *Please don't arrest me; I haven't done anything.* A rush of memories floods through my brain, and I'm watching a replay of all the bad things I've ever done. The time I stole a candy bar. The time I punched someone. The time I smoked a joint. *Am I going to jail?*

Two of the blue people appear next to me, but I can't make my eyes focus on their faces. "Hey, we're going to get you home" *What? Home?* I can't make my mouth form full words; instead, I mumble out something incoherent. There's a hand on my arm now, helping me out of the chair. Anne and the kids are nowhere to be seen. I can hear Karen upstairs yelling about something. I'm being ushered out the door when I finally get my voice back. "Wait! Can I pack my stuff?"

The two officers stop and exchange a confused look. *I guess they didn't think I would need anything.* The same one that spoke before nods "Sure, where is that?" I point behind them and step forward. When I walk between the pair of men, I catch a glimpse of a silver badge, the word 'Federal Marshal' etched into its face. *Aren't they up there with the FBI? I need my bag in case I need to run.*

We make it up the two flights of stairs, and much to my annoyance, both officers follow me into my room. *Jeez, a little privacy, guys.* I start collecting my belongings from around the room. Clothes get crumpled up and shoved into my polka dot duffle bag, followed by pictures, souvenirs, and a pair of headphones. I carefully stack my books in my backpack before turning to a tall dresser by the bed. Before I can open the bottom drawer, I hear pounding footsteps down the hall. *Shit.*

My heart starts racing, and the instinct to run screams at me. I tear open the drawer and pull out my passport, birth certificate, and a full envelope, slamming the drawer shut again quickly. Before I can hide my hand full of documents, they're being yanked away.

The world goes slow and blurry again. *No! I need those! Give them back!* I'm screaming mentally, but my tongue's gone soft too, and I can't make a sound. I watch as my passport and birth certificate are examined and discussed by three different people. Halfway through their debate, the room quiets. I turn and look at the door, watching as a tall, slender woman walks in. She's wearing a suit; her light brown hair is tied back in a low ponytail. She looks like every stereotypical female cop on TV. I'm still frozen in place when she approaches me. "Hey Alaina, my name is

Detective Anderson. I'm here to take you to your parents. Are you ready to go?" It takes a moment to find my words. I want to say '*My parents? They don't want me. Take me somewhere else. Anywhere else.*' Instead, I stutter out, "I need my passport."

The detective looks up at another officer holding everything I had pulled from the drawer and looks back at me. "I'm sorry, kiddo, those have to go to the police station." *Oh, ok.*

*****

A very long five minutes later, I'm walking back down the stairs, followed by the uniform-clad troupe. The detective walks directly behind me. She's talking about something, but I zoned out somewhere between 'no passport' and 'your mom will be happy to see you.'

She's full of shit. Linda doesn't want me. Neither does Simar. Otherwise, they would have come to get me a year ago. Or at least asked where I was. This isn't how things should be. I'm supposed to be starting school. Anne actually cares now.

We walk back into the basement, and I see Anne standing in front of the fireplace. A cop on either side of her. The kids are at the end of the room, sitting on a bench. Karen is leaning against a wall opposite Anne, also flanked by uniforms. I can see Anne's mouth moving, but I can't process what she's saying. We move past her and walk towards the door, which stands wide open. *It looks like a portal to the stars.*

As we step into the night, the cold outside air hits my face, and my mental fog lifts. I can move my tongue and speak. The numbness leaves my fingertips, and I realize that I'm cold. While Detective Anderson and I walk towards a small, dark grey sedan, the band of police officers, federal marshals, and FBI agents disperse behind us.

Anderson walks in front of me and opens the passenger door wide. I throw my duffel bag into the footwell and flop down onto the warm seat. The door closes as the seatbelt glides over my shoulder and clicks it into place. The Detective settles into the driver's seat, types something on a mounted laptop, then starts the car. She turns and looks at me, both hands on the wheel. "You ready to see your family?"

Am I ready?

It takes me a moment to speak. When the words finally come, I'm surprised by what slips out.

"I don't want to go."

END OF BOOK ONE.

RESOURCES

Mental Illness is a serious issue. If you or someone you know has a mental illness, is struggling emotionally, or has concerns about their mental health, please use these resources to find help.

National Suicide Prevention Lifeline: 1-800-273-8255

Crisis Text Line: Text HELLO to 741741

Disaster Distress Helpline: 1-800 985-5590

If you or someone you know has run away from home or are homeless, whether youth or adult, please seek crisis intervention. Help is out there.

National Runaway Safeline: 1-800-786-2929

600,000 people go missing in the United States each year. If someone you know has gone missing, call 911 immediately. Further assistance can be found from these resources.

National Center for Missing & Exploited Children: 1-800-843-5678

Association of Missing and Exploited Children's Organizations: 320-363-0470

National Missing and Unidentified Persons System: 855-626-7600

The resources provided here are valid in the United States as of November 17th, 2020, original publication date of this book.

Acknowledgements

I want to say thank you to Stephen and Brian, without your idea of writing a book or screenplay, I never would have given this manuscript a second thought; to Dolly, for seeing the story itching to escape my mind, and helping coax it out. A huge thank you to my wonderful cousin and supportive friends for letting me hash out my life multiple times over the years. Without you, I would have never dug most of my memories from the layers of PTSD they were buried in. Most of all, I want to thank Matt, for always having my back and pushing me to follow my dreams. I love you more than words can say, and I always appreciate your support (even when I can't articulate that).

CONTINUE THE STORY AT

www.byalainadavis.co

Made in the USA
Las Vegas, NV
16 December 2020